...lished
...ands,
...avel.

...our
...ets
...rld,
...ffers a wealth of
...nce and a passion for travel.

**Rely on Thomas Cook as your
travelling companion on your next trip
and benefit from our unique heritage.**

Thomas Cook **pocket** guides

GENEVA

Written by Kerry Walker, updated by Teresa Fisher

Published by Thomas Cook Publishing
A division of Thomas Cook Tour Operations Limited
Company registration no. 3772199 England
The Thomas Cook Business Park, Unit 9, Coningsby Road,
Peterborough PE3 8SB, United Kingdom
Email: books@thomascook.com, Tel: +44 (0) 1733 416477
www.thomascookpublishing.com

Produced by Cambridge Publishing Management Limited
Burr Elm Court, Main Street, Caldecote CB23 7NU
www.cambridgepm.co.uk

ISBN: 978-1-84848-432-0

© 2007, 2009 Thomas Cook Publishing
This third edition © 2011 Thomas Cook Publishing
Text © Thomas Cook Publishing
Maps © Thomas Cook Publishing/PCGraphics (UK) Limited
Transport map © Communicarta Limited

Series Editor: Karen Beaulah
Production/DTP: Steven Collins

Printed and bound in Spain by GraphyCems

Cover photography © Iconotec/Alamy

CONTENTS

SYMBOLS KEY
The following symbols are used throughout this book:

🅐 address 🕿 telephone 🅦 website address 🅔 email
🕒 opening times 🅝 public transport connections ❶ important

The following symbols are used on the maps:

🔢 information office		▪ point of interest	
✈ airport		O city	
➕ hospital		O large town	
🛡 police station		○ small town	
🚍 bus station		═ motorway	
🚆 railway station		─ main road	
✝ cathedral		─ minor road	
❶ numbers denote featured		─ railway	
cafés & restaurants			

Hotels and restaurants are graded by approximate price as follows:
£ budget price **££** mid-range price **£££** expensive

❶ *Geneva's giant Floral Clock*

INTRODUCING
Geneva

Introduction

Geneva is like a huge Swiss chocolate box, where each experience should be savoured: from the hum of life in the medieval Old Town to the pin-drop peace of the lake front, where the early morning mist peels back to reveal Mont Blanc. On the surface this city is silky smooth, with its five-star hotels, plush boutiques and gourmet haunts – but appearances can be deceptive. Bite beneath the surface and you'll get an explosion of different experiences.

Most surprising, perhaps, is the proximity of nature to the city, and the variation of its forms. Within spitting distance of the mighty UN headquarters, you can take a ride across Europe's largest Alpine lake, its contours carved out by glaciers, sip home-grown Pinot Noir in vine-clad Satigny, spot pink flamingos in the Jardin Botanique and whoosh down the French Alps on a pair of skis. And with promenades hugging the water's edge, this is one place you won't want to be without your walking boots.

This city of 186,000 inhabitants may be small, but it thinks big. The Cathédrale St-Pierre towers above the cobbled Old Town, the 140-m (460-ft) Jet d'Eau fountain creates a rainbow with its spray and the enormous Horloge Fleurie (Floral Clock) raises eyebrows in the Jardin Anglais. If you want to indulge in culture, you can take your pick: contemporary masterpieces at MAMCO, Monet at the Musée d'Art et d'Histoire and opera highs at the Grand Théâtre.

South of the centre, Carouge steals the Little Italy award with its low-slung Piedmont skyline, shady squares and kooky boutiques. A trip to the Left Bank brings you to the boho cafés and funky bars in Plainpalais, while on the Right is Pâquis – a knot of narrow streets where restaurants whip up world flavours and the hip crowd hangs out on the pier. Like all good chocolate boxes, Geneva really does offer something for everyone.

🔺 *Statuesque beauty in Mon Repos Park*

When to go

SEASONS & CLIMATE

Geneva has a temperate climate, but being surrounded by mountains makes it temperamental too – the northerly *bise* wind from the Alps can make it feel chilly and it occasionally snows as late as March and April. However, spring gradually becomes mild, and summers are warm but not too hot, peaking at around 25°C (77°F).

In autumn, expect a final burst of colour in Geneva's parks and the odd shower; it is the ideal time to explore the city's galleries and enjoy leisurely strolls. Winters occasionally bring light snow, with temperatures hovering between 5°C (41°F) and a frosty –2°C (28.4°F).

Note that during long holidays such as Christmas and Easter, many shops, restaurants and museums remain closed over the whole period.

ANNUAL EVENTS
February & March
Geneva Carnival Costumed parades, streams of colourful floats, music, dancing, parties and street entertainment bring carnival fever to Geneva for the three days in February or March that lead up to Ash Wednesday.

International Motor Show The city steps up a gear in spring when the motor-mad check out the latest in cars, technology and accessories at this mammoth exhibition held at the Palexpo. ⓐ Palexpo Exhibition Centre ⓣ 022 761 11 11 ⓦ www.salon-auto.ch

April & May

AMR Jazz Festival Jazz, soul and blues rhythms at the Alhambar draw music lovers to Geneva in droves. ⓐ 10 rue des Alpes
ⓣ 022 716 56 30 ⓦ www.amr-geneve.ch

Geneva Marathon Thousands of runners cover a scenic route through the city. ⓐ Place des Nations ⓣ 022 787 07 53
ⓦ www.genevemarathon.ch

◗ *A game of chess in Parc des Bastions*

June

Bol d'Or Mirabaud Regatta Europe's largest sailing regatta on inshore waters, with over 500 boats racing from Geneva's Port Noir to Le Bouveret at the eastern end of Lake Geneva and back. ☎ 022 707 05 00 ⓦ www.boldor.ch

Fête de la Musique Streets and squares are transformed into open-air stages for this monster music festival, staging everything from *chanson* to jazz and pop concerts. ☎ 022 418 65 32 ⓦ www.ville-ge.ch/culture/fm

July & August

Fêtes de Genève Parades, fireworks and late-night parties make this festival a highlight in Geneva's summer calendar and have drawn well over two million visitors a year. Best of all, it's free! ☎ 022 909 70 00 ⓦ www.fetes-de-geneve.ch

Musiques en Été From classical concerts to funky jazz, sopranos to African beats, this two-month festival breathes musical life into the city. ☎ 022 418 36 18 ⓦ www.ville-ge.ch/culture/musiques

OrangeCinema Catch the latest flicks on a giant, open-air screen at this summer film festival by the lake. ⓦ www.orangecinema.ch

September

La Bâtie Festival A celebration of dance, theatre and music across the city. ☎ 022 738 19 19 ⓦ www.batie.ch

Fête des Vendanges Taste the produce of the grape harvest in the nearby village of Russin. As well as free-flowing wine, this intoxicating festival features markets, music and street entertainment. ⓦ www.russin.ch

November & December

Christmas Market The twinkling market on place de la Fusterie has stalls with handmade crafts, gingerbread and mulled wine. ⓐ Place de la Fusterie ❶ Tourist office: 022 909 70 70

Christmas Ice Rink Warm up with mulled wine and raclette after a stint on the ice. ⓐ Place du Rhône ❶ Tourist office: 022 909 70 70

Coup de Noël A teeth-chattering 125-m (137-yd) swim in Lake Geneva. ⓐ Jardin Anglais ❶ Tourist office: 022 909 70 70 ⓦ www.gn1885.ch

Festival Arbres & Lumières Well-known artists decorate Christmas trees with lighting displays, transforming Geneva into a city of spectacular light. ⓦ www.arbresetlumieres.ch

Fête de l'Escalade History is revisited at this must-see event celebrating the city's victory in 1602 in riotous fashion (see page 14). ❶ 022 312 37 39 ⓦ www.1602.ch

PUBLIC HOLIDAYS

New Year's Day 1 Jan

Good Friday 6 Apr 2012, 29 Mar 2013, 18 April 2014

Easter Sunday 8 Apr 2012, 31 Mar 2013, 20 April 2014

Easter Monday 9 Apr 2012, 1 Apr 2013, 21 April 2014

Ascension Day 17 May 2012, 9 May 2013, 29 May 2014

Whit Monday 28 May 2012, 20 May 2013, 9 June 2014

Swiss National Day 1 Aug

Geneva Fast 7 Sept

Christmas Day 25 Dec

Restauration Genèvoise 31 Dec

Escalade

Fanfare parades, festive revelry and a whole lot of Swiss chocolate smashing make the Escalade the most important event of the year. Held on the weekend closest to 11 December, the unique celebrations commemorate the city's 1602 victory over the Duke of Savoy's troops, who tried to attack Geneva by scaling the city's walls at night. Genevan Catherine Cheynel, better known as the Mère Royaume, stopped some of the attackers dead in their tracks by pouring a pot of scalding vegetable soup over their heads – her determined resistance helped secure Geneva's independence.

The week before the big event, there's a race called the Course de L'Escalade, where hundreds of sprightly locals turn out to stampede through the Old Town's narrow streets to Parc des Bastions – a fun way to keep fit and take in the sights. Many of the runners wear flamboyant costumes.

On the following weekend, festivities build up to Sunday's torchlit parade; this marks the historical event with re-enactments complete with 17th-century costume and artillery demonstrations. As darkness falls, drummers, pipers and trumpeters march past, musketeers on horseback open fire and brave swordsmen display their skills. The noise is ear-splitting and the atmosphere electric. The parade winds through the cobbled Old Town to Cathédrale St-Pierre, where visitors can warm up with mugs of the infamous vegetable soup and spicy *vin chaud* (mulled wine).

The event culminates with the ritual smashing of the *marmite* (cooking pot). The difference is that today's pots are made of chocolate and filled with marzipan vegetables. The shelves of every *pâtisserie* and *confiserie* in Geneva stock these traditional treats, which should be shattered with a single blow (preferably not over someone's head): a sweet end to an ill-fated invasion.

◯ *Marzipan vegetables commemorate an ancient victory*

History

Geneva has seen its fair share of incomers throughout its long and turbulent history, stretching back to 3000 BC when Celtic tribes first settled on the banks of Lake Geneva. The Romans conquered the town in 120 BC and the first written mention of 'Genua' was by Julius Caesar around 52 BC.

The year AD 350 marked a turning point in Geneva's history as Germanic Burgundians occupied the town and bishops took power there, making it their first capital in 443. Less than a century later, Franks stepped in and Geneva became part of the Merovingian Kingdom. In the 9th century, the Burgundian Kingdom retook the reins of power until 1032, when the last King of Burgundy died, at which point the German Empire took over.

Geneva blossomed in the Middle Ages and made its mark on the map with the growing importance of its trade fairs, underpinned by the *combourgeoisie*, an alliance which strengthened the bonds between Geneva, Bern and Fribourg. The Protestant Reformation played a pivotal role in shaping the city and was finally accepted by the people in 1536. Just three years later, one of the key figures in the movement, Jean Calvin, founded the city's college and academy.

At the beginning of the 17th century, attention turned to Savoy, which had for some time posed a threat to Geneva's independence. On the night of 11 December 1602, the Duke of Savoy's troops attempted once again to attack the city by climbing its walls using ladders. But they were driven away by the inhabitants, in an event that is celebrated annually at the Escalade (see page 12).

The 18th century spelt a golden age for Geneva, as the watchmaking industry and banking sector flourished. Among the city's inhabitants at this time was famous writer and philosopher Jean-Jacques Rousseau, whose writings, proclaiming universal liberty and equality, sowed the seeds of the French Revolution. In 1798, Geneva was annexed to France, but regained its freedom in 1813 after the defeat of Napoleon.

A year after Henry Dunant established the Red Cross in 1863, the Geneva Convention was signed, calling for the protection of victims of war and conflict. These milestones laid the foundations for humanitarian law and explain why Geneva was chosen as the headquarters of the League of Nations in 1919. After World War II, Geneva became established as the European headquarters of the United Nations and boomed economically and socially. Despite the current recession, which hit Geneva later than many European cities, it continues to play a fundamental role in world affairs, with its ever-growing crop of international organisations, a prosperous service sector and a high standard of living.

◆ *The Reformation Wall: figures who shaped the city*

Lifestyle

Life and style: Geneva has both in abundance, so it's no coincidence that this Swiss city continually ranks high in the yearly Worldwide Quality of Living Survey (usually just behind big brother Zurich, which is usually in first or second place). A glance around reveals a clean, safe city with an excellent infrastructure, booming business and a superb range of chic restaurants and bars in which the hard-working residents love to play. You'll instantly

● Markets are part of Geneva's appealing mix

feel at home in this welcoming, cosmopolitan city, which is posh but not pretentious, attractive but not overblown, efficient but by no means dull.

The first thing that strikes you is Geneva's relaxed pace of life. With cheery locals who are happy to converse and cars that stop to let you cross the road, this feels a million miles away from the hustle and bustle of most metropolises. This laid-back atmosphere is undoubtedly influenced by the lake, the city's natural escape valve, which is surrounded by beautiful parks and dramatic mountain panoramas. Despite their Rolex watches and passion for champagne, Genevans are well-groomed country kids at heart. With the Alps on their doorstep for skiing in winter and beaches for swimming in summer, it's no wonder they go to work with a spring in their step.

With its mixture of languages and cultures, Geneva is a multi-ethnic melting pot. Genevans tend to have an open-minded attitude and liberal streak. Here, businessmen in smart suits share coffee with penniless poets, while Rastafarians and Portuguese bakers hang out with politicians at the Bains des Pâquis. Beneath the Swiss upper crust lies the world in miniature. Adding a dash of energy to the mix is the lively student population that accounts for the plethora of trendy cafés, ever-evolving art scene and late-night partying in high doses.

The good life is what most people associate with Switzerland and it's certainly true of Geneva, a city that epitomises *joie de vivre*. While locals work hard, they are also experts at enjoying themselves, which is why this grown-up playground is dedicated to every possible pastime – from casinos to wining, shopping to alfresco dining. So relax and savour this extraordinary city.

Culture

In many senses, Geneva is the cultural heart of Switzerland. No fewer than 30 world-class museums, as well as scores of galleries, theatres, concert halls and live music venues, have established this city's international reputation for the arts. And culture here is as much about the present as the past: alive and everywhere. Whenever you visit, there's bound to be something raising the cultural barometer, whether on the stage, screen or canvas, from soulful rhythms at the AMR Jazz Festival (see page 9) to fancy footwork at La Bâtie Festival (see page 10).

It doesn't matter where you go in Geneva: you can't escape music. If you're seeking classical highs, it has to be place Neuve, home to the Grand Théâtre (the spitting image of Opéra Garnier in Paris), where the acclaimed Orchestre de la Suisse Romande performs, and the rococo-style Victoria Hall, where strings and

ART OF THE ORDINARY

Causing a ripple of excitement in the Swiss art world, Geneva-born artist John M Armleder frequently displays his unique and intriguing work at MAMCO. Art in the ordinary is what his exhibitions are about, bringing together abstract paintings, sculpture, drawings and photos to depict the beauty of the banal. A prime example is furniture art, where tables and chairs are splashed with colour, suggesting that we're inspired by not only art, but also by what surrounds it.

◆ *Absorbing culture at the Musée d'Art et d'Histoire*

sopranos raise the roof. At the top of the alternative music tree, innovative venues such as L'Usine, Salle Centrale and Le Chat Noir regularly host jam sessions and concerts from live jazz to world music, techno and rock.

Geneva has more than its fair share of excellent galleries that will satisfy the cravings of art buffs. At the top of the list is the Musée d'Art et d'Histoire, showcasing everything from prehistoric artefacts to masterpieces by Rodin and Konrad Witz. Housed in a former factory, MAMCO is its contemporary contender with its attention-grabbing temporary exhibitions.

Other art gems include the Musée Ariana, which covers the entire spectrum of ceramics and glassware, and the Musée Rath, housing an exceptional fine-arts collection. Those who prefer their art outdoors should check out the wacky Schtroumpfs building on the Right Bank, with irregular lines, vivid colours and mosaic patterns that would give Gaudí a run for his money.

The stage has its part to play in Geneva's cultural life, too, with everything from classic to avant-garde productions. For high-quality ballet, opera and theatrical performances, book tickets for the Grand Théâtre or catch cutting-edge drama at the Comédie de Genève. The Théâtre du Grütli is a sound choice for improvised and quirky plays, while Théâtre de Carouge hosts a mix of experimental productions and timeless favourites. L'Usine is the city's darling of the daring and features an adventurous line-up and performances that always cross the boundaries of convention.

● *Discover centuries' worth of ceramics at the Musée Ariana*

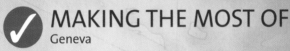 # MAKING THE MOST OF
Geneva

Shopping

Geneva makes no secret of its love for the finer things in life: markets piled high with the freshest produce, chocolatiers making mouths water with Swiss truffles and fashion designers showing off the latest trends.

Geneva's shops are open year-round, six days a week. Shopping hours are generally 09.00–19.00 Monday to Saturday, with smaller boutiques often closing for lunch. Major shopping malls and department stores stay open for late-night shopping until 21.00 on Thursdays.

Whether you're determined to shop till you drop or simply fancy a bit of window-shopping, every corner of Geneva offers something different. Sniff out the latest styles in the boutiques and high-street stores that pepper the Left Bank. For luxury brands, head for the diamond-encrusted rue du Rhône and rue de la Confédération, where glitzy creations in jewellers like Cartier and Bulgari come with a matching price tag. Carouge is the place to buy one-off crafts, from hand-thrown pots to pralines.

Malls and department stores are also abundant in this shoppers' paradise – something especially welcome in bad weather. Conveniently located near the station, Metro Shopping Cornavin is lined with high-street names like Swarovski, Lacoste and Yves Rocher. Nearby, the six-level Manor department store is the ideal one-stop shop, tempting shoppers to spend on fashion, fragrances and home design. Go to the top floor for panoramic views over Geneva. Slightly more upmarket, Globus on rue du Rhône is well stocked with everything from funky footwear to gourmet flavours in the basement food court.

⏺ *Masses of choice in Geneva's chocolate shops*

USEFUL SHOPPING PHRASES

How much is this?
C'est combien?
Seh combyahng?

Can I try this on?
Puis-je essayer ceci?
Pweezh ehssayeh serssee?

My size is ...
Ma taille (clothes)/
ma pointure (shoes) est ...
*Mah tie/mah
pooahngtewr eh ...*

I'll take this one, thank you
Je prends celui-ci/
celle-ci, merci
*Zher prahng serlweesee/
sehlsee, mehrsee*

If you're bargain hunting or looking to fill up your picnic basket, head to one of Geneva's morning markets. Stalls brim with local produce such as fruit, flowers, cheese, honey and handmade breads every Wednesday and Saturday at Carouge's food market (🕐 07.30–14.00). While you're roaming the square, pause to taste freshly baked pastries, drink local wines and soak up the relaxed village atmosphere. On the same days, antique enthusiasts hunt for gems at the Plainpalais Flea Market (🕐 08.00–18.00), crammed with bric-a-brac, musty books, vintage clothes and old vinyl.

It's not hard to find Swiss-made products and quality souvenirs. Multi-purpose, classic red Victorinox army knives always make a useful gift. For a lingering taste of Geneva, buy a gift-wrapped box of Zeller's divine truffles or Philippe Pascoët's basil-infused pralines (if they last till you get home ...). It wouldn't be Switzerland without Swatch – pick up arty watches at the store on rue du Mont-Blanc.

Eating & drinking

Geneva excels in the gastro department with hearty fare like cheese fondue and rösti on the menu. Dining here doesn't have to be expensive: virtually every restaurant has a good-value *plat du jour* that caters for the budget conscious. So whether you want to reach for the Michelin stars on the quai du Mont-Blanc, eat your way around the world in Pâquis, or snuggle up in a wood-panelled bistro, this city has the place for you.

Do a quick check on your budget and appetite before choosing which area of the city to eat in. Big on character and Swiss staples, the cobbled streets of the Old Town are stacked with cosy brasseries and Alpine-style chalets serving dishes such as entrecôte steak and fondue. Many offer good-value lunch specials. Go underground to vaulted cellars where candles flicker, or pull up a chair on the terrace of a *petit bistro* on the place du Bourg de Four for alfresco dining in summer.

For those with a bigger bank balance, the swish restaurants lining the glitzy quai du Mont-Blanc and quai Wilson beckon. This is the place to enjoy haute cuisine, five-star service and prime views of Lake Geneva. Departing every Thursday and Friday,

PRICE CATEGORIES

The restaurant price guides used in this book indicate the approximate cost of a three-course meal for one person, excluding drinks, at the time of writing.

£ up to CHF50   ££ CHF50–100   £££ over CHF100

fondue cruises offer a more affordable slice of luxury on the lake.
Ⓦ www.cgn.ch

Tired of cheese and chocolate? Head for Pâquis to savour
world flavours. This hip corner of Geneva spices things up with
everything from feisty Mexican enchiladas to hole-in-the-wall
Moroccan oases. With a distinctly multicultural edge, you'll be able
to indulge in Lebanese, Thai, Japanese and Portuguese specialities.

Low-key Carouge has plenty of intimate, rustic bistros serving
Swiss fare with a Mediterranean twist. Once a Sardinian enclave,
the love of all things Italian persists: think antipasti, wood-fired
pizza, risotto and fresh fish.

🔺 Why not go for a picnic in one of Geneva's many parks?

One of the cheapest and most pleasant dining options in summer is an alfresco picnic. Geneva has a string of attractive parks and gardens that are perfect for a picnic when the weather permits. Top choices include the Jardin Anglais and Bains des Pâquis pier, where you can lay your blanket by the lake front and drink in views of the Jet d'Eau, or munch your lunch beside the rhododendrons in the flower-strewn Jardin Botanique. In a city that loves its food, there is no shortage of *pâtisseries*, *fromageries* and wine shops from which to fill your basket either!

Geneva has plenty of restaurants serving international food, but you mustn't leave without trying the delicious local specialities. Alpine heartiness meets French finesse in Geneva's kitchen, where fresh, locally sourced ingredients are used. Fondue is a perennial favourite and lots of fun – skinny forks are used to dip bread into a bubbling pot of cheese or fruit into thick hot melted chocolate. Another tasty winter warmer is rösti (grated potatoes with onion and bacon). Carnivores should tuck into *longeole* (unsmoked pork sausage flavoured with cumin and fennel) or try *l'assiette valaisanne* (cold meat platter). Other specialities to look out for include lake perch, creamy Tomme cheese and artichoke-like cardoons.

WALKING ON CHOCOLATE

Chocolate is a firm favourite in Geneva, and every chocolatier sells the speciality of the city, *pavés glacés*. The brainchild of the 19th-century confectioner Henri Auer, these creamy chocolates shaped like cobblestones simply melt in your mouth.

Surrounded by vine-clad hills, Geneva is wine country, producing some excellent varieties including crisp Chasselas whites, full-bodied Gamay reds and fruity Pinot Noirs. Those who want to taste the grape where it is grown should make for the wineries in nearby Russin and Satigny.

Tipping is optional in Switzerland. Nearly all restaurants in Geneva include a service charge of 15 per cent, but it's normal to leave a small tip if you are pleased with the service. Locals tend to round off the bill to the nearest few francs or tip between five and ten per cent. In Switzerland, it's standard practice to give the tip direct to the waiter.

USEFUL DINING PHRASES

I would like a table for ... people
Je voudrais une table pour ... personnes
Zher voodray ewn tabl poor ... pehrson

May I have the bill, please?
L'addition, s'il vous plaît?
L'adission, seel voo pleh?

Waiter/waitress
Monsieur/Mademoiselle
M'syer/madmwahzel

Does it have meat in it?
Est-ce que ce plat contient de la viande?
Essker ser plah kontyahng der lah veeahngd?

Where is the toilet, please?
Où sont les toilettes, s'il vous plaît?
Oo sawng leh twahlet, seel voo pleh?

Entertainment & nightlife

As the sun sets over Mont Blanc, neon lights and twinkling fountains illuminate the lake. While Geneva may not seem wild on the surface, dig deeper and you'll find it has more than enough after-dark action to keep night owls happy. With a lively student population that just wants to have fun, and a plethora of ultra-cool lounge bars and underground clubs vying for your attention, this city knows how to let its hair down.

Variety is the spice of Geneva's nightlife – think divas, dressed up to the nines, sipping cocktails on the quai du Mont-Blanc, and locals unwinding over a glass of red wine on a terrace in the Old Town; arty types hanging out in Plainpalais bars and fashionistas sharing the dance floor in place de la Fusterie. From grunge to glitz, roulette to reggae, fine wines to perfect pints, Geneva will entertain you.

A night in Geneva begins in typically relaxed fashion with a good meal in one of the Old Town's wood-panelled brasseries and a few drinks on the quai du Mont-Blanc. Things pick up around 23.00 as bars lining the Pâquis, Plainpalais and the city centre fill with high-spirited revellers, and the music is turned up a notch. If you want to shake your booty in one of the hottest clubs in town, don't get there until after midnight.

Geneva's clubbing scene moves from students bopping to urban beats to glamour-pusses sipping champagne as they strut their stuff. Check out the ultra-chic B Club and Gold & Platinum (you might just get in if you look the part), Café Cuba, where partygoers sway to Latino rhythms, and 7ème Ciel for house music and mojitos. One of the most popular clubs for

● *As darkness descends, Geneva lights up*

young people and students is **Alhambar** (ⓐ 10 rue de la
Rôtisserie ⓣ 022 312 13 13 ⓦ www.alhambar.com).

If you're after some more relaxed night-time entertainment,
head to one of Geneva's many pubs and bars. The buzzing place
du Bourg de Four is the place for alfresco drinking and people-
watching in summer. For snug British-style pubs with no frills,
a laid-back feel and Guinness® on tap, make for the Grand Rue
or rue de Lausanne. The Plainpalais district around rue Bovy-
Lysberg and place du Cirque is the Left Bank's hip heart, serving
up Zen-style lounge bars where the cocktails are creative,
grooves mellow and crowds effortlessly cool.

If you're seeking trendy rather than traditional, you'll
get your kicks in the multicultural Pâquis on the Right Bank.
Clustered here are hole-in-the-wall bars playing everything
from soul to salsa, and the vibe is very much come as you are.
While this is Geneva's red-light district, it's unlikely you'll feel
threatened walking here at night.

Whether you're into sopranos and strings, jazz or comedy, the
performing arts are alive and well in Geneva. Classical concerts,
opera and dance raise the roof on the place Neuve, which is
dominated by the acclaimed Grand Théâtre and Conservatoire

WHAT'S ON
Geneva Agenda An online booklet on the Geneva Tourism
website gives up-to-date listings of events in Geneva.
ⓦ www.geneve-tourisme.ch
Info Concert Find the latest festival, concert, theatre and
cinema listings on this French site. ⓦ www.infoconcert.com

de Musique. For a more offbeat experience, make for funky
Le Chat Noir in Carouge, which reels in the crowds with live jazz
and jam sessions in the cellar. The Arena (Ⓦ www.geneva-arena.ch)
is the place for everything from stand-up comedy to musicals
and rock concerts.

To book tickets in advance, contact the venue direct or try
Billetnet (Ⓦ www.billetnet.ch), which covers major festivals,
gigs and performances.

🔺 *The Grand Théâtre dominates place Neuve*

Sport & relaxation

SPECTATOR SPORTS

With a capacity of 30,000, **Stade de Genève** (ⓐ 16 route des Jeunes ⓘ 022 827 44 00 ⓦ www.servettefc.ch ⓝ Bus: 21, 22, 42, 43, 48 to Stade de Genève) is home to the city's biggest football club, Servette, and was a host stadium for the 2008 European Championship.

The multi-purpose arena at Geneva's huge **Palexpo Exhibition Centre** (ⓐ Route François-Peyrot, Grand-Saconnex ⓘ 022 761 11 11 ⓦ www.palexpo.ch ⓝ Bus: 5 to Palexpo), situated next to the airport, hosts a number of top sporting events including the Showjumping World Cup.

PARTICIPATION SPORTS
Adventure Center

From kayaking the rapids of the Arve River to paragliding from Mont Salève, this professional centre has 50 years' experience and offers bags of white-knuckle thrills. There are guides for the inexperienced or you can hire craft if you prefer to head off on your own adventure. ⓐ 8 quai des Vernets ⓘ 079 213 41 40 ⓦ www.rafting.ch ⓛ Apr–Oct ⓝ Tram: 15, 17 to Acacias

Swimming

Make a splash from the Bains des Pâquis pier, or go to Geneva's brilliant beach. **Genève-Plage** (ⓐ Port Noir, quai de Cologny ⓘ 022 736 24 82 ⓦ www.geneve-plage.ch ⓛ 10.00–20.00 daily (May–mid-Sept) ⓝ Bus: 2, E, G to Genève-Plage ⓘ Admission charge) is set in a large park on the lake edge, and has an

Olympic-sized pool, water slides, diving boards, volleyball, basketball and children's activities.

Watersports
The **Wake Sport Center** (ⓐ 9 quai de Cologny ❶ 079 202 38 73 ⓦ www.wake.ch ❹ May–mid-Sept ⓝ Bus: 2, E, G to Genève-Plage) next to Geneva's beach provides waterskiing, wakeboarding, wakeskating and hydrofoiling.

RELAXATION
Cruise
Swissboat (ⓐ 4–8 quai du Mont-Blanc ❶ 022 732 47 47 ⓦ www.swissboat.com ⓝ Bus: 29 to Chantepoulet) offers an array of relaxing mini-cruises to take in the sights, as well as trips along the River Rhône.

Mont Salève
Take the *téléphérique* (cable car) to Geneva's nearest mountain, the 1,380-m (4,527-ft) Mont Salève, where you can hike or mountain bike in summer and cross-country ski in winter. ⓐ Veyrier ❶ (+33) 04 50 39 86 86 ⓦ www.telepheriquedusaleve.com ❹ Check website for times ⓝ Bus: 34, 41 to Veyrier-École; 8 to Veyrier-Douane

Rousseau Island
Named in honour of philosopher Jean-Jacques Rousseau, this tranquil island in the Rhône is a great place to relax or enjoy a bite to eat at the island's restaurant with its stunning panoramic views. ⓐ Pont des Bergues ⓦ www.geneve-tourisme.ch

Accommodation

Swiss hotels are notoriously pricey, but in Geneva it is still quite possible to find central hotels that won't break the bank. There's also a good range of character accommodation available in the city, including Swiss-chalet, belle-époque, feng-shui-inspired and boutique-style hotels. The city's hostels offer great value for solo travellers, while campers can enjoy prime lake views in beautiful surroundings.

HOTELS

Hôtel Admiral £–££ This mid-range hotel offers smart rooms decorated in warm hues. Perks include free Wi-Fi Internet and a hearty breakfast. ❸ 8 rue Pellegrino Rossi (Right Bank) ❶ 022 906 97 00 Ⓦ www.hoteladmiral.ch Ⓝ Train: Gare de Cornavin

Hôtel Bel'Espérance ££ A central, no-frills hotel. All rooms have satellite TV and the terrace has views over the city's rooftops to Lake Geneva. ❸ 1 rue de la Vallée (Left Bank) ❶ 022 394 33 00 Ⓦ www.hotel-bel-esperance.ch Ⓝ Bus: 8 to Rive

> **PRICE CATEGORIES**
> The ratings below indicate the approximate cost of a room for two people for one night in Geneva, including breakfast.
> **£** up to CHF150 **££** CHF150–250 **£££** over CHF250

Hôtel Bernina ££ Conveniently located opposite the station, this hotel has basic but spotless rooms that won't blow the budget, all with cable TV, safe and soundproofed windows. **a** 22 place de Cornavin (Right Bank) **t** 022 908 49 50 **w** www.bernina-geneve.ch **N** Train: Gare de Cornavin

Hôtel de Genève ££ A stone's throw from Geneva's key sights, this belle époque hotel scores points for its homely feel. The wood-panelled reception recalls an Alpine chalet and the 39 rooms are well kept. **a** 1 place Isaac-Mercier (Right Bank) **t** 022 908 54 00 **w** http://hotel-de-geneve.ghix.com **N** Tram: 15, 16 to Isaac-Mercier

Hôtel des Tourelles ££ Overlooking the Rhône, this charming hotel has attractive, high-ceilinged rooms with soft drapes and hardwood floors. Free Wi-Fi. **a** 2 boulevard James-Fazy (Right Bank) **t** 022 732 44 23 **w** www.destourelles.ch **N** Tram: 13 to Cornavin

Hôtel Royal ££–£££ Contemporary chic sums up this smart hotel offering 24-hour room service, free Wi-Fi Internet access and on-site parking. After a long day of sightseeing, unwind in the *hammam* and sauna, or enjoy drinks by the fireside in the lounge. **a** 41–43 rue de Lausanne (Right Bank) **t** 022 906 14 14 **w** www.manotel.com **N** Tram: 13, 15 to Môle

Hôtel d'Angleterre £££ Central, old-fashioned and refined, with individually decorated rooms, impeccable service and a lakeside setting by the Jet d'Eau. **a** 17 quai du Mont-Blanc (Right Bank)

◔ *Wallow in luxury at the Hôtel Royal*

☎ 022 906 55 55 **ⓦ** www.dangleterrehotel.com **Ⓝ** Tram: 13, 14 to place de la Navigation; Bus: 1 to place de la Navigation

Hôtel Edelweiss £££ Reminiscent of a traditional Swiss chalet, this hotel brings the mountains to the heart of Geneva. The snug rooms have all mod cons including free Wi-Fi access. **ⓐ** 2 place de la Navigation (Right Bank) **☎** 022 544 51 51 **ⓦ** www.manotel.com **Ⓝ** Bus: 1 to place de la Navigation

Hôtel Jade £££ Earthy tones create a sense of calm in this feng-shui-inspired hotel near the lake. Free Wi-Fi access. **ⓐ** 55 rue Rothschild (Right Bank) **☎** 022 544 38 38 **ⓦ** www.manotel.com **Ⓝ** Tram: 13 to Butini

Hôtel Longemalle £££ With high ceilings, dark wood floors and ornate flourishes, this hotel epitomises belle époque elegance. The attractive rooms offer minibar, cable TV and Internet access. **ⓐ** 13 place de Longemalle (Left Bank) **☎** 022 818 62 62 **ⓦ** www.longemalle.ch **Ⓝ** Bus: 27 to place du Port

Hôtel Tiffany £££ This turn-of-the-century boutique hotel is a real find; the plush rooms all have squeaky-clean bathrooms. Relax in the wood-panelled lounge, book a massage and wake up to an excellent breakfast. **ⓐ** 20 rue de l'Arquebuse (Left Bank) **☎** 022 708 16 16 **ⓦ** www.hotel-tiffany.ch **Ⓝ** Tram: 16 to Stand

HOSTELS

City Hostel £ Near the main station, this offers single, double and dorm beds. The rooms are clean and there's a communal

kitchen, lockers, a TV room and Internet access. ⓐ 2 rue Ferrier
(Right Bank) ☏ 022 901 15 00 ⓦ www.cityhostel.ch Ⓝ Tram: 13
to Môle

YH Geneva £ The pick of the budget bunch, this bright and
modern hostel, 1 km (²/₃ mile) from the city centre, has clean
and comfortable shared dorms. The good facilities include a
laundry, snack bar, Internet access and library. Breakfast is
included. ⓐ 30 rue Rothschild (Right Bank) ☏ 022 732 62 60
ⓦ www.yh-geneva.ch Ⓝ Tram: 13, 15 to Butini

CAMPSITES

Camping Pointe à la Bise £ Enjoy breakfast on the beach at this
lake-front site, ten minutes' drive from Geneva. The campsite
has shady pitches, and facilities include a swimming pool, bike
hire, restaurant and shop. ⓐ 18 chemin de la Bise, Vésenaz ☏ 022
752 12 96 ⓦ www.campingtcs.ch Ⓛ Apr–Sept Ⓝ Bus: E to La Bise

Camping du Val de l'Allondon £ Situated in a nature reserve,
this peaceful campsite is just a short train ride from the centre.
ⓐ 106 route de l'Allondon, Satigny ☏ 022 753 15 15 Ⓛ Apr–Oct
Ⓝ Train: Satigny

THE BEST OF GENEVA

There's plenty to enjoy in Geneva, but these are the sights that should really not be missed.

TOP 10 ATTRACTIONS

- **Cathédrale St-Pierre (St Peter's Cathedral)** Scale the North Tower's spiral staircase and see Geneva shrink (see page 58).

- **Bains des Pâquis** Hang out with the hip crowd on the Right Bank's pier (see page 74).

- **MAMCO (Museum of Contemporary Art)** Contemporary art is on the menu at this funky Left Bank gallery (see page 66).

- **Le Chat Noir** The cat's out of the bag – this club is the coolest place in Carouge (see page 99).

- **Jet d'Eau (Water Fountain)** This 140-m (460-ft) fountain rises like a vision above Lake Geneva (see pages 62 & 64).

- **Musée d'Art et d'Histoire (Art & History Museum)** This cavernous museum has everything from paintings by Monet to Egyptian artefacts (see page 66).

- **Horloge Fleurie (Floral Clock)** Created from 6,500 flowers, this celebrates the Swiss tradition of watch- and clock-making (see page 58).

- **Palais des Nations (Palace of Nations)** Take a tour of this political powerhouse (see page 78).

- **Jardin Botanique (Botanic Gardens)** Mediterranean blooms and pink flamingos vie for attention at these gorgeous lake-front gardens (see page 75).

- **Musée International de la Croix-Rouge et du Croissant-Rouge (International Red Cross & Red Crescent Museum)** The work of the world's most famous humanitarian organisation is explored at this fascinating museum (see page 81).

🔽 *The view from the cathedral platform*

Suggested itineraries

HALF-DAY: GENEVA IN A HURRY

Kick off your stay with a whirlwind tour of the hilltop Old Town, winding through narrow streets to take in key sights like the arcaded Town Hall (see page 62) and turreted Maison Tavel (see page 66). Pause at the medieval Cathédrale St-Pierre (see page 58) to climb the North Tower for giddying views over the city's rooftops and lake. Before you leave, be sure to glimpse the flower-strewn Horloge Fleurie and dancing Jet d'Eau from the manicured lawns of the Jardin Anglais (see page 62).

1 DAY: TIME TO SEE A LITTLE MORE

A stroll along the lake front brings you to the vibrant Bains des Pâquis pier (see page 74), where (weather permitting) you can take a quick dip or drink in views of snow-clad Mont Blanc over a coffee. Further along, you'll reach Mon Repos villa and the beautiful Jardin Botanique (see page 75), where pink flamingos wade. Back on the Left Bank, munch on rösti beneath the Taverne de la Madeleine's beams (see page 69), then head for the Musée d'Art et d'Histoire (see page 66) to admire Van Gogh masterpieces and the famous Konrad Witz altarpiece.

2–3 DAYS: TIME TO SEE MUCH MORE

Scratch the city's surface to find lesser-known treasures – from cutting-edge exhibitions at MAMCO (see page 66) to the lofty Mur des Réformateurs in the Parc des Bastions (see page 64). After taking a tour of the Palace of Nations (see page 78), pop across to the International Red Cross Museum (see page 81), which tells a moving tale of triumph and tragedy. Next up, Carouge beckons, with its Sardinian-style houses, pavement cafés and kooky boutiques that are a world away from the buzzing centre. As night falls, catch quirky performances at L'Usine (see page 73) or a live music act at Carouge's Le Chat Noir (see page 99).

LONGER: ENJOYING GENEVA TO THE FULL

Once you've devoured all Geneva has to offer, get a taste for the surrounding region. Cross the Franco-Swiss border to Annecy (see page 114), where canals lead to the red-turreted medieval castle. Here you can try your hand at mountain climbing or drift away on the lake's translucent waters. Stepping east, enjoy the delights of the Olympic city of Lausanne (see page 102) – from the Gothic heights of Notre-Dame Cathedral via the art gems gracing the walls of the grand Palais de Rumine to the relaxed vibe on the waterfront promenade of Ouchy.

⬤ *Lake Geneva's Left Bank or* rive gauche

Something for nothing

Switzerland has quite a reputation for being expensive, so it's pleasing to discover that some of the best things in Geneva are free. First up is a whirlwind tour of the Old Town that won't cost you a penny (or a Swiss franc, to be precise), where an amble takes in sights such as the arcaded Hôtel de Ville (see page 62), frescoed Tour du Molard (see page 65) and the medieval Cathédrale St-Pierre (see page 58) – step inside to admire the magnificent rose window. Wind through narrow cobbled streets to the water's edge, where the Horloge Fleurie (see page 58) keeps ticking and the Jet d'Eau fountain turns heads (see pages 62 & 64).

For a free taste of local life, head for the shady Parc des Bastions (see page 64), where people congregate to play chess on giant boards and the Mur des Réformateurs commemorates key figures of the Reformation. In summer, bring your swimming togs and take a dip from Bains des Pâquis pier (see page 74). This may be a city, but there's plenty of country about: explore Geneva's patchwork of greenery by strolling the Right Bank's promenade. From here you can glimpse sculpture-strewn gardens and gaze at one of the city's most striking sights – the sun setting over Mont Blanc. You can easily spend the afternoon wandering through the vast Jardin Botanique (see page 75), home to cacti, fragrant plants and deer.

If all that exercise has made you thirsty, be sure to pick up a leaflet from the tourist office giving a comprehensive list of wineries offering free tastings every Saturday. For the cost of a bus ticket, you could vine-hop your way around the winegrowing villages of Anières, Céligny, Russin and Satigny. It costs nothing to get your cultural fix in many of Geneva's intoxicating galleries and museums. Art buffs should make a beeline for the Musée d'Art et d'Histoire (see page 66) to brush up against Rembrandts and Roman treasures, or the sublime Musée Ariana (see page 80) to gawp at precious porcelain. Savvy travellers time their visit to coincide with the first Sunday of the month, when most museums are free, including the must-see MAMCO (see page 66) and Musée Rath (see page 67).

⬥ *Musée Ariana: see the ceramic collection for free*

When it rains

When the rain comes, Geneva shines, with a host of indoor activities to help you forget about the wet weather. If you feel like hibernating, the Old Town has a glut of cosy cafés and low-beamed bistros that are just the ticket. And no country does comfort food like the Swiss – everything seems much brighter over a mug of real hot chocolate or a *caquelon* (a type of pot) filled with cheese fondue to warm your cockles. When the heavens open, the arty cafés around Plainpalais are a great place to hang out with a bottomless cup of coffee and a good book.

Undercover shopping can be the ultimate pick-me-up when it rains. To escape sudden showers, scoot into Globus (see page 68) on rue du Rhône to immerse yourself in the latest styles and tasty specialities in the basement food court. A stone's throw from Carouge, modern **La Praille** mall (ⓣ 022 304 80 00 ⓦ www.la-praille.ch) shelters 80 high-street shops selling everything from prune juice to pralines, plus tea rooms, restaurants and a bowling alley.

Culture can compensate for dull skies too. Go down instead of up at the cathedral to view centuries-old foundations at the archaeological site (see page 58). A few paces away, the medieval Maison Tavel (see page 66) traces Geneva's history with elaborate art and artefacts. Immerse yourself in contemporary creations at MAMCO (see page 66), then pop over to the elegant Musée Patek Philippe (see page 66) to gawp at Art Nouveau timepieces. Escape heavy downpours at the heart-rending Musée International de la Croix-Rouge et du Croissant-Rouge (see page 81) to learn more about the humanitarian work of this international organisation.

It may be too nippy for a dip in the lake, but that's all the more excuse to test out the state-of-the-art *hammam* and sauna complex at the Bains des Pâquis (see page 74). A long steam in the Turkish bath or a soothing massage will leave you feeling as fresh as a daisy. If you've got cash to splash, the ultimate boost on a drizzly day is a trip to the exclusive La Réserve spa (see page 82), which has a huge range of feel-good therapies to chase away rainy-day blues.

🔺 *Discover the latest styles and unusual gifts at Globus*

On arrival

TIME DIFFERENCE

Switzerland runs on Central European Time (CET), which is an hour ahead of Greenwich Mean Time (GMT). Daylight saving applies: clocks are put forward one hour at the end of March and back one hour at the end of October, on the same day as in the UK.

ARRIVING

By air

A major international hub, **Aéroport Genève-Cointrin** (☎ 022 717 71 11 🅦 www.gva.ch) is 5 km (3 miles) from the centre. See page 126 for details of airlines that operate from the airport.

The modern airport offers an excellent range of facilities open seven days a week, including shops, cafés, ATMs, car hire, a post office, bureau de change, supermarket and pharmacy.

A train shuttles passengers between the airport and Geneva's main station in just six minutes (trains depart every twelve minutes). Alternatively, you can take bus number 10 into town, which departs roughly every ten minutes. The Unireso information desk in the arrivals hall provides tickets and details of routes and timetables.

A taxi to the centre will set you back a minimum of 30–35 Swiss francs, depending on the time of day, the number of passengers and surcharges.

By rail

Swiss Federal Railways (☎ 0900 300 300 🅦 www.sbb.ch) is renowned for its efficiency and comfort, and operates a regular

IF YOU GET LOST, TRY ...

Do you speak English?
Parlez-vous anglais?
Pahrlay-voo ahnglay?

Is this the way to ...?
C'est la bonne direction pour ...?
Seh lah bon deerekseeawng poor ...?

Can you point to it on my map?
Pouvez-vous me le montrer sur la carte?
Poovehvoo mer ler mawngtreh sewr lah kart?

service to Swiss cities including Lausanne (45 minutes), Bern (two hours) and Zurich (three hours), in addition to French destinations like Lyon (two hours) and Paris (three hours).

The main train station, **Gare de Cornavin** (ⓐ Place de Cornavin ⓣ 0900 300 300 ⓦ www.sbb.ch), is located on the Right Bank and has a good range of facilities including left luggage, a bureau de change and a post office.

By road

Long-distance buses and international coaches arrive at the city's central bus station, **Gare Routière** (ⓐ Place Dorcière ⓣ 022 732 02 30 ⓦ www.gare-routiere.ch). For comprehensive information on coach excursions and bus transfers to French ski resorts, see the 'Ticket Reservation' section of the above website.

Geneva is well connected to the rest of Switzerland and Europe via the A40 (L'Autoroute Blanche) to the French Alps, the A42 to Lyon, and the A1 to Lausanne. For the centre, follow the signs for Genève-Lac and the route de Lausanne. Although

Geneva

0   800 metres
0   800 yards

Lausanne

Genève-Cointrin

N

ROUTE DE LA VOIE

ROUTE DE MEYRIN

MEYRIN

AVENUE LOUIS CASAÏ

ROUTE DE MEYRIN

AUTOROUTE A1

ROUTE DE VERNIER

AVENUE DU PAILLY

VERNIER

TUNNEL DE VERNIER

Le Rhône

AVENUE DE CHÂTELAINE

ROUTE DU BOIS-DES-FRÈRES

AVENUE DE L'AIN

ROUTE D'AIRE

AVENUE D'AIRE

CH. DES SELLIÈRES

Cimetière de Saint-Georges

Bois-de-la Batie

AUTOROUTE A1

RUE DE LOEX

AVENUE DES GRANDES-COMMUNES

ROUTE DU PONT-BUTIN

ROUTE DE CHANCY

LANCY

BERNEX

TUNNEL DE CONFIGNON

ROUTE DE CHANCY

ONEX

Gare de la Praille

ROUTE DU GRAND-LANCY

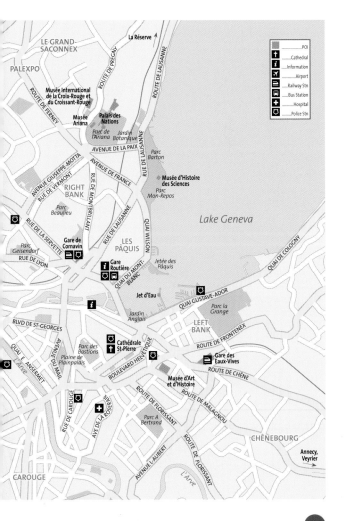

driving in Geneva is relatively hassle-free compared with other major cities, parking can be expensive and difficult to find. Plan in advance by checking the location of multi-storey and Park & Ride car parks on ⓦ www.geneve.ch. The speed limit is strictly observed in Switzerland and, for motorway driving, you should display a *Vignette* (toll sticker) in the windscreen at all times.

FINDING YOUR FEET

You will soon feel at home in Geneva, a cosmopolitan city with a laid-back feel and a pedestrianised Old Town. Many locals are fluent in English and happy to direct travellers.

As Geneva is a safe city with a low crime rate, it's unlikely you'll experience any problems during your stay, but it's always wise to keep an eye on your valuables and be careful if walking through dimly lit, less-populated areas at night.

● *The action in Geneva centres around the lake*

OLD TOWN TOURS
Jump aboard a traditional mini road train for a tour around the Old Town. The 45-minute tour covers Geneva University, Cathédrale St-Pierre and La Statue Pictet de Rochemont, with guides explaining the history behind the sights. Other tours offered include a panoramic trip around the hills of Geneva to see the Jet d'Eau, Floral Clock, Grange Park and Brunswick Monument. Tours depart from place du Rhône and quai du Mont-Blanc. **STT Trains Tours** ❶ 022 781 04 04 ⓦ www.sttr.ch

ORIENTATION
Hemmed in by the Alps and straddling the Franco-Swiss border, Geneva is located in Switzerland's southwest corner. Split in two by the snaking River Rhône, the city hugs the banks of Lake Geneva and is framed by mountains.

Most of the action centres around the lake: the UN institutions, Jardin Botanique and Les Pâquis on the Right Bank, and Cathédrale St-Pierre, the Jet d'Eau fountain and the Plainpalais on the Left. Carouge is just south of the centre.

GETTING AROUND
Geneva's efficient public transport network makes it simple to get around. All visitors staying in a hotel, youth hostel or campsite are entitled to a free Geneva Transport Card from the tourist office for unlimited use of the city's trams, buses, boats and trains for the duration of their stay.

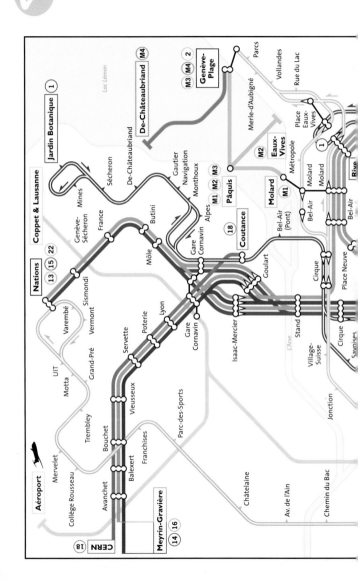

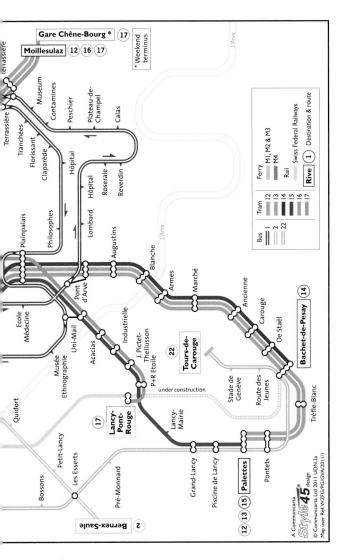

Gare Chêne-Bourg * (17)
Moillesulaz (12)(16)(17)
*Weekend terminus

Terrassière
Terrassière
Tranchées
Florissant
Claparède
Philosophes
Plainpalais
Ecole Médecine
Uni-Mail
Musée Ethnographie
Quidort
Petit-Lancy
Bossons
Les Esserts
Pré-Monnard

Museum
Contamines
Peschier
Plateau-de-Champel
Calas
Hôpital
Hôpital
Lombard
Roseraie
Reverdin
Pont d'Arve
Augustins
Acacias
Industrielle
J. Pictet-Thellusson
P+R Etoile
Lancy-Mairie
Grand-Lancy
Piscine de Lancy

Blanche
Armes
Marché
Ancienne
Carouge
De Staël
Tréfle-Blanc
Pontets

Tours-de-Carouge (22)

Stade de Genève
Route des Jeunes

under construction

Bachet-de-Pesay (14)

Lancy-Pont-Rouge (17)

Palettes (12)(13)(15)

L'Arve
L'Arve

Bernex-Saule (2)

Legend:

Ferry
M1, M2 & M3 — M1, M2 & M3
M4 — M4

Rail
Swiss Federal Railways

Rive (1) Destination & route

Tram
12
13
14
15
16
17

Bus
1
2
22

A Communicarta
Style45 design
© Communicarta Ltd 2011 UDN 2a
Map user Ref:WZFiGPG/GWA/2011/1

Trams are one of the fastest and most reliable ways to get about the city. Geneva's tram lines criss-cross the city and operate from around 06.00 to 24.00. Each stop has a ticket machine (you'll need exact change). Geneva's bus network also operates from 06.00 to 24.00 with a night service at weekends. You'll find bus and tram route maps and timetables at each stop. Alternatively, call 🕿 0900 022 021 or see 🔵 www.tpg.ch

Geneva encourages pedal power, and from late April to late October bikes can be borrowed for free. For details, contact **Genève Roule** (🕿 022 740 13 43 🔵 www.geneveroule.ch).

With so much water, it's often convenient to get around Geneva by boat. Pick a cruise or simply hop aboard one of the yellow bus-boats (*mouettes*) that shuttle passengers every ten minutes between Pâquis, Eaux-Vives and place du Molard. Information is available on 🕿 022 732 29 44 🔵 www.mouettes genevoises.ch

Car hire

Geneva's excellent public transport network means you can get around easily. However, if you're planning on going further afield, hiring a car could be a good option. All of the following car hire companies have outlets at the airport.

Avis 🕿 022 929 03 30; Also at 🅐 44 rue de Lausanne 🕿 022 731 90 00 🔵 www.avis.com

Budget 🕿 022 717 86 75 🔵 www.budget.com

Europcar 🕿 022 717 81 10 🔵 www.europcar.com

Hertz 🕿 022 717 80 80 🔵 www.hertz.com

🔵 *Committed to peace: a statue near the Palais des Nations*

THE CITY OF
Geneva

Left Bank

If you're looking for variety, Geneva's Left Bank will not disappoint: from the medieval Old Town in the shadow of the cathedral spires to the glittering lake front, where the Floral Clock ticks, and the Plainpalais and its ultra-cool bars. Whether you want to chill in shady parks, wallow in modern art, gorge on fondue or boutique-shop along Grand Rue, you can graze for days on the Left Bank's riches.

SIGHTS & ATTRACTIONS

Cathédrale St-Pierre (St Peter's Cathedral)

The medieval monolith rises like a vision above Geneva's Old Town. The edifice is a fusion of Romanesque, Gothic and neoclassical styles – step inside to admire its cross-ribbed vaulting and huge rose window. Underground is an archaeological site that traces the cathedral's early foundations. But if you're seeking highs, climb the North Tower's steep spiral staircase to view the bell tower and spires. The terrace affords bird's-eye views over the city's rooftops, lake and mountains. ❸ Place St-Pierre ❶ 022 319 71 91 ⓦ www.saintpierre-geneve.ch ❷ 09.30–18.30 Mon–Sat, 12.00–18.30 Sun (June–Sept); 10.00–17.30 Mon–Sat, 12.00–17.30 Sun (Oct–May) ❷ Bus: 36 to Cathédrale ❶ Admission charge (North Tower)

Horloge Fleurie (Floral Clock)

A living tribute to a country that runs like clockwork, this blooming beautiful clock in the Jardin Anglais will have you reaching for

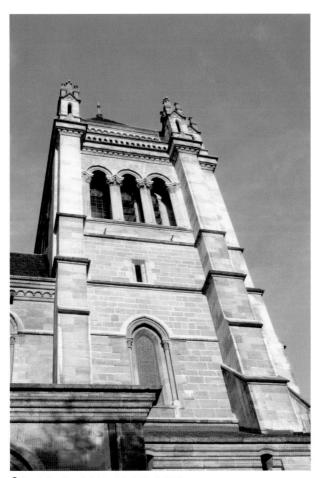

⬤ *Reach the dizzy heights at Cathédrale St-Pierre*

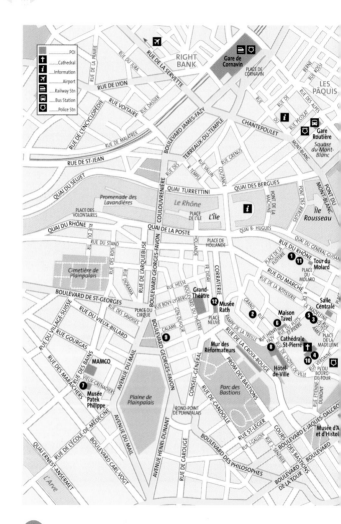

POI
Cathedral
Information
Airport
Railway Stn
Bus Station
Police Stn

RUE DE LA PRAIRIE
RUE DU JURA
RUE DE LA SERVETTE
RIGHT BANK
Gare de Cornavin
PLACE DE CORNAVIN
BERNE
RUE ROSSI
RUE DE LYON
RUE VOITAIRE
RUE DASSIER
LES PÂQUIS
RUE DES ALPES
RUE PECOLAT
RUE DE L'ENCYCLOPÉDIE
RUE DE MALATREX
BOULEVARD JAMES-FAZY
CHANTEPOULET
Gare Routière
MONT-BLANC
RUE DE ST-JEAN
TERREAUX-DU-TEMPLE
RUE GRENUS
RUE VALLIN
R. TEMPLE
COUTANCE
Square du Mont-Blanc
QUAI DU SEUJET
QUAI TURRETTINI
QUAI DES BERGUES
PONT DU MONT-BLANC
Promenade des Lavandières
Le Rhône
PLACE DE L'ÎLE
L'Île
Île Rousseau
PONT DE LA MACHINE
PONT DES BERGUES
PLACE DES VOLONTAIRES
QUAI DU RHÔNE
QUAI DE LA POSTE
QUAI B.-HUGUES
COULOUVRENIÈRE
PLACE DE HOLLANDE
HOLLANDE
QUAI DU GÉNÉRAL-GUISAN
RUE DU RHÔNE
RUE DE LA ROTISSERIE
RUE DU STAND
RUE DES ROIS
TIR
RUE DE L'ARQUEBUSE
RUE HESSE
FR. DIDAY
CORRATERIE
PLACE DE LA FUSTERIE
RUE DE LA CONFÉDÉRATION
11 Tour du Molard
PLACE DU MOLARD
RUE DU MARCHÉ
Cimetière de Plainpalais
RUE DES SAVOISES
RUE BOVY-LYSBERG
BOULEVARD GEORGES-FAVON
GRAND'RUE
RUE DU PERRON
Grand-Théâtre
12 Musée Rath
2
GRAND'RUE
Maison Tavel **1**
Salle Centrale
5 3
BOULEVARD DE ST-GEORGES
PLACE DU CIRQUE
CALAME
9
PLACE NEUVE
RUE DE LA TREILLE
RAMPE DE LA TREILLE
RUE HENRI-FAZY
RUE DU PUITS-ST-PIERRE
PLACE DE LA MADELEINE
RUE DU VILLAGE-SUISSE
RUE DU VIEUX-BILLARD
Mur des Réformateurs
Cathédrale St-Pierre **8** **4** **10**
RUE DE LA CROIX-ROUGE
RUE DE L'HÔTEL-DE-VILLE
RUE DU SOLEIL-LEVANT
RUE GOURGAS
RUE DES BAINS
VIEUX-GRENADIERS
Hôtel-de-Ville
RUE ÉTIENNE-DUMONT
RUE DU BOURG-DE-FOUR
MAMCO
AVENUE DU MAIL
CONSEIL-GÉNÉRAL
PROM. DES BASTIONS
7 Musée Patek Philippe
RUE DES MARAICHERS
AVENUE HENRI-DUNANT
Parc des Bastions
RUE DE CANDOLLE
Plaine de Plainpalais
ROND-POINT DE PLAINPALAIS
RUE ST-LÉGER
RUE DE L'ÉCOLE-DE-MÉDECINE
BOULEVARD CARL-VOGT
AVENUE DU MAIL
RUE DE CAROUGE
BOULEVARD DES PHILOSOPHES
RUE J. GAILLOUX
COURS DES BASTIONS
BOULEVARD E.-JAQUES-DALCROZ
Musée d'A et d'Histoi
QUAI ERNEST-ANSERMET
L'Arve
BOULEVARD DES BASTIONS DE LA TOUR

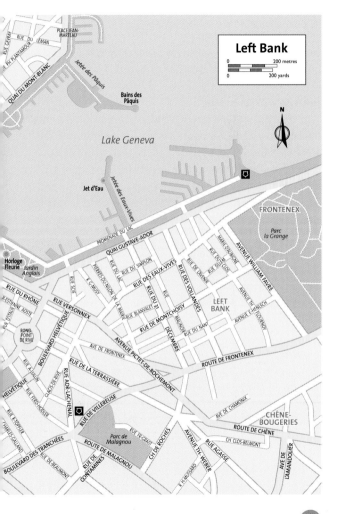

your camera. Around 6,500 brightly coloured flowers and plants are used to create new displays each spring and autumn to celebrate Switzerland's famous watch-making industry. ➌ Jardin Anglais, quai du Général-Guisan ⓝ Bus: 27 to place du Port

Hôtel de Ville (Town Hall)

With its arcades overlooking a cobbled inner courtyard, Geneva's town hall has been the cogs and wheels of the city's political life since the 15th century and is still the seat of the cantonal government. Just opposite, take a peek at the Old Arsenal, a former granary with impressive cannons and mosaic frescoes depicting historical scenes. ➌ Rue de l'Hôtel-de-Ville ⓝ Bus: 36 to Hôtel de Ville

Jardin Anglais (English Garden)

This ever-so-English garden is laced with paths that pass dancing fountains, statues and a bandstand. Find a shady spot beneath the oak trees, take a cruise on the lake or wander along

WATERWORKS

Now the focal point of the lake, Geneva's famous Jet d'Eau was originally just a security valve. Over the years the locals grew quite attached to this huge fountain – one of the largest in the world. Today it shoots around 250 litres (55 gallons) of water per second into the sky and, when the sun shines, creates a rainbow that can best be admired from the Pont du Mont-Blanc bridge.

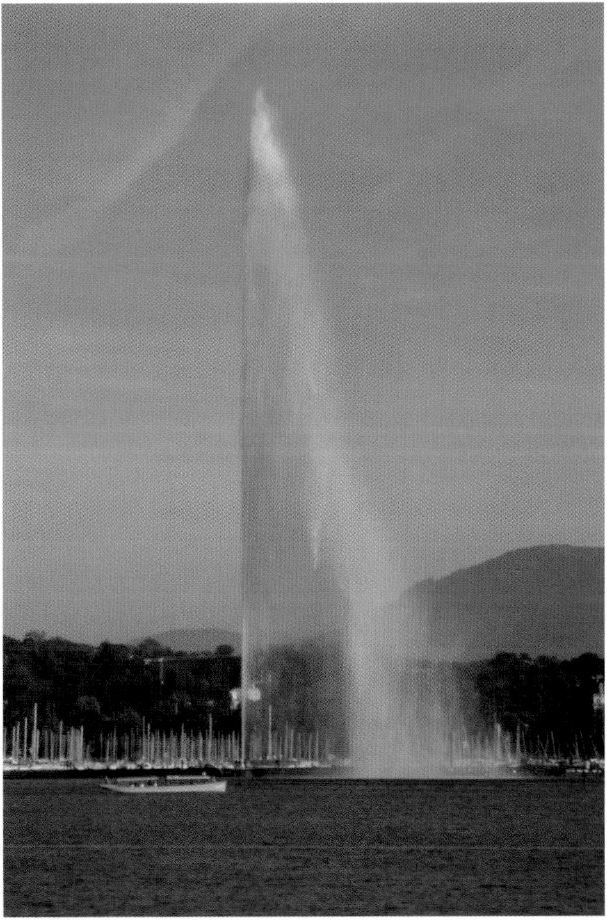

Splashing success: the Jet d'Eau

the front for uninterrupted views of the fountain. In summer, the park is awash with magnolias. Quai du Général-Guisan Bus: 27 to place du Port

Jet d'Eau (Water Fountain)

Perhaps Geneva's most iconic landmark, this eye-catching 140-m (460-ft) fountain cascades into Lake Geneva at a speed of 200 km/hour (124 mph) and looks particularly striking illuminated by night or during one-off light shows. It is best seen from quai du Général-Guisan. ⏱ 09.00 or 10.00–dusk daily (Mar–Nov); 11.30–16.00 (Dec–Feb) ⊗ Bus: E, G to Eaux-Vives

Mur des Réformateurs (Reformation Wall)

This breathtaking, 100-m (330-ft) wall was built in 1909 to commemorate the 400th anniversary of Jean Calvin's birth and the 350th anniversary of the Academy of Geneva. Set against a backdrop of bas-reliefs are four larger-than-life sculptures that represent the key figures of the 16th-century Reformation. ⓐ Parc des Bastions, off rue de la Croix-Rouge ⊗ Tram: 12, 17 to place Neuve

Parc des Bastions

Originally part of the city's fortifications, this park is where locals come to jog along the tree-lined avenue, play chess on giant boards, relax in the sunshine and while the afternoon away. This central pocket of greenery is home to one of the main university buildings, a popular café-restaurant and the awe-inspiring Reformation Wall. ⓣ Café: 022 310 86 66 ⊗ Tram: 12, 17 to place Neuve

Tour du Molard (Molard Tower)

Once part of the city's defence walls, today this red-turreted tower is dwarfed by the centre's taller buildings. Glance up to see its frescoes, clock face and coat of arms. ⓐ Place du Molard ⓝ Tram: 16 to Molard

CULTURE

Grand Théâtre (Opera House)

Dominating place Neuve, this grand 19th-century opera house has earnt an international reputation for its world-class opera, theatre, ballet and recitals. The season runs from October to May. ⓐ 11 boulevard du Théâtre ⓣ 022 418 31 30 ⓦ www.geneve opera.ch ⓝ Tram: 12, 17 to place Neuve

▲ *Chill out with the locals*

Maison Tavel

Set in the city's oldest medieval residence, this fascinating museum features displays of antique furniture, tapestries and silverware spanning the Middle Ages to the 20th century. Be sure to look at the model of pre-1850 Geneva. ⓐ 6 rue du Puits-St-Pierre ☎ 022 418 37 00 ⓦ www.ville-ge.ch/mah 🕒 10.00–17.00 Tues–Sun ⓝ Bus: 36 to Hôtel de Ville ❶ Free; admission charge for temporary exhibitions

MAMCO (Museum of Contemporary Art)

This former factory is now the driving force behind Geneva's contemporary art scene, presenting fresh and edgy temporary exhibitions that focus on artists like John M Armleder and a broad variety of media. ⓐ 10 rue des Vieux-Grenadiers ☎ 022 320 61 22 ⓦ www.mamco.ch 🕒 12.00–18.00 Tues–Fri, 11.00–18.00 Sat & Sun ⓝ Bus: 1 to École-Médecine ❶ Admission charge

Musée d'Art et d'Histoire (Art & History Museum)

A must-see for culture vultures, this cavernous museum covers fine arts, archaeology and applied arts, presenting everything from Egyptian antiquities to Roman pottery and medieval weaponry. Art lovers should head straight for the permanent collection of masterpieces from the likes of Rembrandt, Monet and Van Gogh. A highlight is Konrad Witz's 15th-century altarpiece. ⓐ 2 rue Charles-Galland ☎ 022 418 26 00 ⓦ www.ville-ge.ch/mah 🕒 10.00–17.00 Tues–Sun ⓝ Bus: 1, 8 to Tranchées

Musée Patek Philippe (Patek Philippe Museum)

A temple to Swiss timekeeping, this opulent museum shelters a peerless collection of antique and Patek Philippe timepieces, from elaborate 17th-century pocket watches to Art Nouveau pendant designs and astronomical clocks. ⓐ 7 rue des Vieux-Grenadiers ❶ 022 807 09 10 ⓦ www.patekmuseum.com ❶ 14.00–18.00 Tues–Fri, 10.00–18.00 Sat ⓝ Bus: 1 to École-Médecine ❶ Admission charge

Musée Rath (Rath Museum)

Housed in a neoclassical building, this fine arts museum showcases the collection of 19th-century benefactor Simon Rath and frequently stages first-rate exhibitions. ⓐ 2 place Neuve ❶ 022 418 33 40 ⓦ www.ville-ge.ch/mah ❶ 10.00–17.00 Tues & Thur–Sun, 12.00–21.00 Wed ⓝ Tram: 12, 17 to place Neuve ❶ Admission charge

Salle Centrale

If you're seeking an alternative cultural scene, this venue screening art-house films and staging experimental productions could be just the ticket. The centre's eclectic programme stretches from flamenco to concerts, exhibitions to improvised plays. ⓐ 10 rue de la Madeleine ❶ 022 311 60 35 ⓦ www.sallecentrale.ch ⓝ Tram: 12, 16 to Molard

RETAIL THERAPY

Boulevard du Vin Sniff out Pinots and Sauvignon Blancs at this sleek cellar where you can taste the wines before you buy. ⓐ 1–3 boulevard Georges-Favon ❶ 022 310 91 90 ⓦ www. boulevard-du-vin.ch ❶ Shop: 10.00–19.00 Mon–Fri; Bar: 11.30–23.00 Mon–Wed, 11.30–24.00 Thur & Fri ⓝ Tram: 15 to Stand

Bucherer Be dazzled by the selection of seductive treasures on view at Switzerland's leading watch and jewellery retailer, naturally located on the city's glitziest shopping street.
🅐 45 rue du Rhône 🕾 022 319 62 66 🅦 www.bucherer.com
🕓 09.00–19.00 Mon–Fri, 09.00–18.00 Sat 🚋 Tram: 16 to Molard

Globus On the main shopping drag, this smart five-level department store has everything a shopaholic could desire: from fashion to sportswear, cosmetics and a glorious food court.
🅐 48 rue du Rhône 🕾 058 578 50 50 🅦 www.globus.ch
🕓 09.00–19.00 Mon–Wed, 09.00–21.00 Thur, 09.00–19.30 Fri, 09.00–18.00 Sat 🚋 Tram: 16 to Molard

Halle-de-Rive Perfect for picnic supplies, this small indoor market contains stalls selling fine cheeses, cold cuts, bread, fruit and vegetables. 🅐 Entrances at 29 boulevard Helvétique and 17 rue Pierre-Fatio 🅦 www.halle-de-rive.com 🕓 07.30–19.00 Mon–Fri, 06.00–16.00 Sat 🚋 Tram: 12, 13 to Rive

Plainpalais Flea Market Eagle-eyed bargain hunters spend the morning rummaging through antiques, vintage clothes, old records, books and bric-a-brac at this atmospheric flea market.
🅐 Plaine de Plainpalais 🕓 06.30–18.00 Wed & Sat 🚋 Tram: 12, 13 to Rond-Point de Plainpalais

Theodora Romance, nostalgia and the scent of lavender drift from this perfumer par excellence, where you'll find signature fragrances like Rosine rose perfumes and Santa Maria Novella eaux de toilette. 🅐 38 Grand Rue 🕾 022 310 38 75

Ⓦ www.parfumerietheodora.ch Ⓛ 10.00–19.00 Tues–Fri, 10.00–18.00 Sat Ⓝ Bus: 36 to Hôtel de Ville

Zeller This dreamy chocolatier has a glass counter full of exquisite pralines, truffles, marzipan creations and melt-in-your-mouth *pavés glacés* (cobblestone-shaped chocolates). It's a secret too sweet to keep … Ⓐ 1 place de Longemalle Ⓣ 022 311 50 26 Ⓛ 08.00–18.45 Mon–Fri, 08.00–18.00 Sat Ⓝ Bus: 8, 27 to place du Port

TAKING A BREAK

Globus au Molard £ ❶ A wide choice of high-quality fast food, served at individual crêpe, noodle, sushi, antipasti and seafood bars to eat in or take away. There is also a wellness bar serving freshly squeezed juices and a wine bar. Ⓐ 48 rue du Rhône Ⓣ 058 578 50 50 Ⓦ www.globus.ch Ⓛ 07.00–22.00 Mon–Fri, 09.00–22.00 Sat Ⓝ Tram: 16 to Molard

Le Rozzel £ ❷ Hobbit-burrow-like windows and a tiny terrace add to the appeal of this crêperie in the Old Town, where you can satisfy your pancake cravings with sweet and savoury varieties. Ⓐ 18 Grand Rue Ⓣ 022 312 42 72 Ⓛ 11.00–18.00 Mon–Sat Ⓝ Bus: 36 to Hôtel de Ville

Taverne de la Madeleine £ ❸ For local flavour and great-value lunches, make for this centuries-old tavern with creaking beams, exposed stone and the hum of chatter. Home-made fare includes dishes like rösti potatoes and perch filet. No alcohol. Ⓐ 20 rue Toutes-Âmes, off place de la Madeleine Ⓣ 022 310 60 70

🕐 07.30–21.00 Tues–Sat, last orders 20.00 (July & Aug);
07.30–18.30 Mon–Fri, last orders 16.00, 09.00–16.30 Sat,
last orders 14.30 (Sept–June) 🚍 Bus: 8, 27 to place du Port

AFTER DARK

RESTAURANTS
Chez Ma Cousine 'On y Mange du Poulet' £ ❹ Spit-roasted
chicken served with mounds of Provençal potatoes is the reason
to visit this rustic, good-value restaurant in the centre of town.
📍 6 place du Bourg-de-Four 📞 022 310 96 96 🌐 www.chezma
cousine.ch 🕐 11.00–23.30 Mon–Sat, 11.00–22.30 Sun
🚍 Bus: 3, 5 to Croix-Rouge

Le Morgan £ ❺ Low ceilings and wood panelling give this vaulted
cellar a cave-like feel. Take a pew to enjoy classic bistro fare in a
warm, friendly setting. 📍 14 rue de la Madeleine 📞 022 311 81 00
🕐 11.30–14.30, 17.00–21.00 Mon–Fri 🚍 Bus: 8, 27 to place du Port

Brasserie de l'Hôtel de Ville ££ ❻ There is an old-world feel about
this bistro with its polished brass and antique-lined walls. The
fare is Swiss with favourites like Geneva-style pork and fondue
on the menu. The terrace comes alive in summer. 📍 39 Grand Rue
📞 022 311 70 30 🕐 07.00–23.30 Mon–Fri, 10.00–23.30 Sat & Sun
🚍 Bus: 3, 5 to Croix-Rouge

Café des Bains ££ ❼ Near the MAMCO, this modern restaurant
dishes up poetry on a plate: think sautéed gambas with prune
chutney and polenta or Kerala curry with cumin-glazed carrots.

ⓐ 26 rue des Bains ⓣ 022 321 57 98 ⓦ www.cafedesbains.com
ⓛ 12.00–14.00, 19.30–22.30 Tues–Sat ⓝ Bus: 1 to École-Médecine

Café Papon ££ ❽ Dine beneath the vaults at this chic restaurant near the Parc des Bastions. Foodies come to mingle and enjoy tender veal and morels in cream sauce. ⓐ 1 rue Henri-Fazy
ⓣ 022 311 54 28 ⓛ 07.00–23.00 Mon–Fri, 09.30–23.00 Sat
ⓝ Bus: 3, 5 to Croix-Rouge

Cave Valaisanne – Chalet Suisse ££ ❾ This cosy rustic restaurant is *the* place in town to tuck into a speciality fondue or some traditional Swiss country fare. ⓐ 23 boulevard Georges-Favon, place du Cirque ⓣ 022 328 12 36 ⓛ 08.00–01.00 ⓝ Tram: 13, 14, 15 to Cirque

Au Pied de Cochon ££ ❿ Pig's trotters are the speciality of this ever-popular brasserie oozing turn-of-the-century charm.
ⓐ 4 place du Bourg-de-Four ⓣ 022 310 47 97 ⓦ www.pied-de-cochon.ch ⓛ 08.00–24.00 Mon–Fri, 11.00–24.00 Sat & Sun
ⓝ Bus: 3, 5 to Croix-Rouge

Senso ££ ⓫ Clean lines, muted tones and brown leather create an ultra-modern setting in which to feast on Italian fusion cuisine. Olive trees provide shade in the inner courtyard. ⓐ 56 bis rue du Rhône ⓣ 022 310 39 90 ⓦ www.senso-living.ch ⓛ 10.00–02.00 Mon–Fri, 17.00–02.00 Sat ⓝ Bus: 29 to Molard

U Bobba Restaurant ££ ⓬ This restaurant celebrates Emilio Bobba, a poet with a passion for gourmet food. The restaurant

is sophisticated but affordable. 21 rue de la Corraterie
022 310 53 40 11.30–15.00 Mon, 11.30–15.00, 18.00–00.30
Tues–Fri, 18.00–01.00 Sat Bus: 3 to Bovy-Lysberg

BARS & CLUBS

Alhambar This vintage-style café by day transforms into a
happening bar by night, with a cool lively crowd and hit parade
dance rhythms. 10 rue de la Rôtisserie 022 312 13 13
www.alhambar.com 12.00–14.00 Mon, 12.00–14.00,
17.00–01.00 Tues & Wed, 12.00–14.00, 17.00–02.00 Thur & Fri,
16.00–02.00 Sat, 11.00–24.00 Sun Tram: 16 to Molard

B Club Bright young things dress up to the nines and head for
this über-cool club to dance till the sun rises. 12 place de la
Fusterie 022 311 05 55 www.lebaroque.ch 23.00–04.00
Thur, 23.00–05.00 Fri & Sat Bus: 1, 10 to Bel-Air

BBM Wine Bar A red cow welcomes you to this little wine bar.
It also has a terrace with lake views and is great for an aperitif.
12 quai du Général-Guisan 022 310 92 36 12.00–15.00,
17.00–02.00 Mon–Sat Bus: 1, 10 to Bel-Air

Café Cuba The crowd is hip, the vibe chilled and the caipirinhas
flow freely. 1 place du Cirque 022 328 42 60 www.cafe
cuba.ch 19.00–01.00 or 02.00 Mon–Fri, 17.00–02.00 Sat
Tram: 15 to Cirque

La Clémence This tiny locals' bar has been in existence since the
city of Geneva was founded. Located at the heart of the Old Town,

it has a charming year-round pavement terrace and serves delicious *vin chaud* (mulled wine) during winter months. ❷ 20 place du Bourg-de-Four ❶ 022 310 70 96 ❸ 06.45–00.30 Mon–Fri, 08.15–01.30 Sat, 07.45–00.30 Sun ❹ Bus: 3, 5 to Croix-Rouge

Demi Lune Café Candles flicker and mellow grooves play at this cosy bar, where you can sink into a sofa and munch tapas with your cocktail. ❷ 3 rue Etienne-Dumont ❶ 022 312 12 90 ❿ www. demilune.ch ❸ 10.00–24.00 Mon–Wed, 10.00–02.00 Thur & Fri, 16.00–02.00 Sat, 12.00–24.00 Sun ❹ Bus: 3, 5 to Croix-Rouge

L'Ethno Bar Everyone who's anyone comes here: students to write, musicians to compose and eco-warriors to plot how to save the world. ❷ 1 rue Bovy-Lysberg ❶ 022 310 25 21 ❿ www. ethnobar.ch ❸ 07.00–02.00 Mon–Fri, 10.00–02.00 Sat & Sun ❹ Tram: 15 to Cirque

Spring Brothers A laid-back pub in the centre of town with Guinness® on tap and big-screen sports. ❷ 23 Grand Rue ❶ 022 312 40 08 ❸ 17.00–02.00 daily ❹ Bus: 3, 5 to place Neuve

L'Usine Urban beats pump out from this trendy venue for alternative arts, housed in a former factory. ❷ 4 place des Volontaires ❶ 022 328 08 18 ❿ www.usine.ch ❸ 12.00–15.00, 17.00–02.00 Mon–Sat ❹ Bus: 10 to Palladium

X-S A cellar-bar-cum-discotheque at the heart of the Old Town. ❷ 19 rue de la Pélisserie, off Grand Rue ❶ 022 311 70 09 ❿ www. xsclub.ch ❸ 23.30–05.00 Fri & Sat ❹ Bus: 3, 5 to place Neuve

Right Bank

Five-star hotels punctuating the quai du Mont-Blanc, crystalline high-rises around the Palace of Nations, boho chic in multicultural Pâquis and gardens hugging the banks of Lake Geneva – the Right Bank has all of this and more. Whether you're seeking the best views of snow-white Mont Blanc, the shade of giant sequoias, a soak in a luxury spa or a mean curry, this district can provide it.

The beauty of the Right Bank lies in its contradictions: from politicians on UN business to Brazilian bartenders in the up-and-coming Pâquis, all-night partying in the Platinum Glam Club to the peace of Mon Repos Park.

SIGHTS & ATTRACTIONS

Bains des Pâquis

With seagulls soaring above, waves lapping against the shore and a lighthouse, this pier in central Geneva wouldn't look out of place at the seaside. This wooden boardwalk is where locals gather for a stroll, coffee or picnic – from sharply dressed business people to students relaxing on the rocks. If you're seeking Geneva's hip side, look no further. It also has beaches from which you can swim – even in winter if you want to give the plucky Genevans a run for their money. There's also a sauna and *hammam* where you can warm up after the big chill. ⓐ 30 quai du Mont-Blanc ⓘ *Hammam*: 022 732 29 74; Café: 022 738 16 16; Massage: 022 731 41 34 ⓦ www.bains-des-paquis.ch ⓛ Café: 08.00–22.30 daily; Sauna: 09.00–21.30 Mon–Sat, 08.00–21.30 Sun; Massage: 10.00–20.00 daily ⓝ Bus: 1 to Pâquis

Brunswick Monument

The architectural equivalent of a wedding cake, this ornate pink-and-white monument is a riot of skinny spires and stone latticework. The mausoleum is the final resting place of eccentric Duke Charles II of Brunswick, who left his entire fortune to Geneva. Frivolous but fun. ❸ Quai du Mont-Blanc Ⓝ Bus: 1 to Monthoux

Jardin Botanique (Botanic Gardens)

You can spend an entire afternoon roaming the city's botanic gardens, which fringe the banks of Lake Geneva. The vast green space features an arboretum, Mediterranean greenhouse and gardens nurturing herbs, vegetables, vines, medicinal plants, magnolias and rhododendrons. There are hands-on displays where it's possible to trace the life cycle of a tree and touch different kinds of bark. As well as plant life, the gardens are home

⬥ The lighthouse at Bains des Pâquis

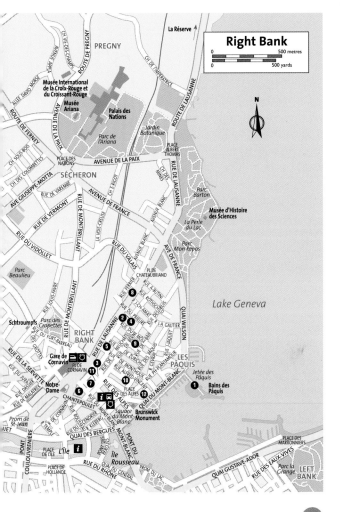

Right Bank

| 0 | | | | | 500 metres |
| 0 | | | | | 500 yards |

N

La Réserve

PREGNY

Musée International
de la Croix-Rouge et
du Croissant-Rouge

Musée
Ariana

Palais des
Nations

Parc de
l'Ariana

Jardin
Botanique

PLACE
ALBERT
THOMAS

Parc Barton

Musée d'Histoire
des Sciences

La Perle
du Lac

Parc
Mon Repos

Lake Geneva

PLACE DES
NATIONS

AVENUE DE LA PAIX

SÉCHERON

Parc
Beaulieu

PL. DE
CHATEAUBRIAND

Schtroumpfs

Parc des
Cropettes

RIGHT
BANK

Gare de
Cornavin

PL. DE
CORNAVIN

Notre-
Dame

LES
PÂQUIS

Jetée des
Pâquis

Bains des
Pâquis

Square
du Mont-
Blanc

Brunswick
Monument

PLACE DES
MARRONNIERS

Prom de
St-Jean

Île
Rousseau

QUAI DES BERGUES

PLACE
DE L'ÎLE

L'Île

QUAI GUSTAVE-ADOR

RUE DES EAUX-VIVES

Parc la
Grange

LEFT
BANK

PLACE DE
HOLLANDE

to parrots, pink flamingos, wild goats and deer. ⓐ 1 chemin de l'Impératrice ⓣ 022 418 51 00 ⓦ www.ville-ge.ch/cjb ⓛ 08.00–19.30 daily (Apr–mid-Oct); 09.30–17.00 daily (mid-Oct–Mar) ⓝ Bus: 1, 11, 28 to Jardin Botanique

Palais des Nations (Palace of Nations)

The immense Palace of Nations is the European headquarters of the United Nations. Colourful flags line the avenue leading up to the huge building. It's worth taking a behind-the-scenes tour to glimpse some of the cavernous halls where the political action takes place. The gardens showcase the symbolic Armillary Sphere, while the enormous *Broken Chair* sculpture stands in the square outside as a protest against landmines. ⓐ 14 avenue de la Paix ⓣ 022 917 48 96 ⓦ www.unog.ch ⓛ 10.00–12.00, 14.00–16.00 daily (Apr–June & Sept–Mar); 10.00–17.00 daily (July & Aug) ⓝ Tram: 13 to Nations

🔽 *A monument to cooperation: the Palais des Nations*

Parc Barton

This English-style landscaped garden is dominated by the pink Villa Barton, which Sir Robert Peel acquired in the 19th century. He planted the forest of giant sequoia trees that still stands tall today. ⓐ 118 rue de Lausanne Ⓝ Bus: 1 to Sécheron

Parc Mon Repos

Centred around a stately 19th-century villa (Casanova is reputed to have stayed in an earlier house on the site), this attractive lake-front park is a pleasant place to walk through. Enjoy the lush Mediterranean gardens, admire snow-capped Mont Blanc and rest in the shade of ancient trees. ⓐ Rue de Lausanne Ⓝ Bus: 1 to Sécheron

La Perle du Lac

With its pretty perennials, mature trees and dancing fountains, this lake-front park is one of Geneva's most scenic spots in which

to relax and soak up the views. A web of paths takes in statues and clipped box hedges. In summer, the lawn is a sea of brightly coloured dahlias. The park is particularly beautiful in late afternoon, when a diffused light turns the Alps various shades of pink.
ⓐ 128 rue de Lausanne Ⓝ Bus: 1 to Sécheron

Schtroumpfs (Smurfs)

While you're unlikely to see any little blue creatures here, this Gaudíesque building named after the Smurfs does indeed look as though it has stepped straight out of a comic strip. Irregular contours, wacky mosaic designs, wave-shaped balconies and larger-than-life mushrooms define this fantastical edifice in Les Grottes. The unconventional icon is one of Geneva's true hidden gems. ⓐ 23–29 rue Louis-Favre Ⓝ Bus: 8 to Grottes

CULTURE

Musée Ariana (Ariana Museum)

Adorned with bas-reliefs and overlooking a beautiful fountain, this museum's pastel-pink façade is wonderfully over the top – visit after dark to see it illuminated. The domed neoclassical building shelters an exquisite collection of ceramics and glasswork spanning seven centuries. ⓐ 10 avenue de la Paix ☎ 022 418 54 50 ✉ ariana@ville-ge.ch 🕙 10.00–17.00 Wed–Mon Ⓝ Bus: 8 to Appia ❶ Free; admission charge for temporary exhibitions

Musée d'Histoire des Sciences (History of Science Museum)

It doesn't cost anything to unravel the wonders of science at this neoclassical mansion set in Perle du Lac park, where you can test out a range of inventions from telescopes and sundials to parabolic mirrors and microscopes. ❸ Villa Bartholoni, 128 rue de Lausanne ☎ 022 418 50 60 🕐 10.00–17.00 Wed–Mon 🚌 Bus: 1 to Sécheron

Musée International de la Croix-Rouge et du Croissant-Rouge (International Red Cross & Red Crescent Museum)

Located opposite the Palace of Nations, this fascinating museum traces the progress of the Red Cross since its foundation in 1863. Multimedia displays take an in-depth look at the world's largest humanitarian network, with themes moving from the 'Written Word', dealing with respect for life, to 'Acts of Mercy', focusing on Florence Nightingale's benevolent deeds. Perhaps most poignant of all is the 'Wall of Time', charting epidemics, tragedies and armed conflicts. ❸ 17 avenue de la Paix ☎ 022 748 95 25 🌐 www.micr.ch 🕐 10.00–17.00 Wed–Mon 🚌 Bus: 8, 28 to Appia ❶ Admission charge

🔺 *The beautiful Villa Bartholoni, home to the Musée d'Histoire des Sciences*

SCINTILLATING SPA
If you fancy a little pampering, head for La Réserve spa. Ranked one of the top retreats in the world, this temple of self-indulgence overlooking Lake Geneva is the playground of celebrities. Signature treatments include balneotherapy, Ayurvedic massage and the 2-hour 40-minute 'Swiss bliss' package. There is an indoor and outdoor pool, a sauna and *hammam* and also a hair salon. It's exclusive and expensive, but the feel-good factor is worthy of the five stars. ⓐ 301 route de Lausanne ⓣ 022 959 59 59 ⓦ www.lareserve.ch ⓛ 06.00–22.00 daily ⓛ Train: Les Tuileries

RETAIL THERAPY

Manor An ideal one-stop shop close to the station, this six-level department store is the biggest in Geneva and stocks women's fashion, fragrances, sportswear, home design, jewellery and lingerie. The top floor affords panoramic views from the terrace.
ⓐ 6 rue de Cornavin ⓣ 022 909 46 99 ⓦ www.manor.ch
ⓛ 09.00–19.00 Mon–Wed, 09.00–21.00 Thur, 09.00–19.30 Fri, 08.30–18.00 Sat ⓝ Tram: 13 to Cornavin

Metro Shopping Cornavin This mall under the station is home to a clutch of high-street stores including Yves Rocher, Swarovski, Lacoste and Merkur for Swiss chocolate. There's also a tea room, bakery, sushi bar and newsagent. ⓐ 30 rue du Mont-Blanc ⓣ 022 900 22 10 ⓦ www.metroshopping.ch
ⓛ 09.00–19.00 Mon–Fri, 09.00–17.00 Sat ⓝ Tram: 13 to Cornavin

Swatch Shop Visit this brightly coloured store for the latest Swatch watches in all shapes and sizes. ⓐ 19 rue du Mont-Blanc ① 022 900 22 10 ① 09.00–19.00 Mon–Fri, 09.00–18.00 Sat ⓝ Bus: 8 to Mont-Blanc

TAKING A BREAK

Bains de Pâquis £ ❶ The tiny café-shack here, part of the outdoor baths on the bank of the river, serves superb breakfasts and one of the finest brunches in town at weekends, with great views of the lake and Jet d'Eau. ⓐ 30 quai du Mont-Blanc ① 022 738 16 16 ⓦ www.bains-des-paquis.ch ① 08.00–22.30 daily (breakfast served until 11.30) ⓝ Bus: 1 to Pâquis

Maison de l'Ancre £ ❷ If you're on a tight budget, this relaxed hospice café serves the cheapest lunch in town – from fresh salads and sandwiches to home-made cakes and coffee. ⓐ 34 rue de Lausanne ① 022 420 58 00 ① 08.00–22.15 Mon–Thur, 08.00–23.15 Fri ⓝ Tram: 13, 15 to Môle

Il Monte Bianco £ ❸ Crammed with the finest Italian fare, from whole hams to wines and olives, the lunchtime queue speaks volumes for the quality. ⓐ 9 rue Chaponnière, off rue des Alpes ① 022 732 41 54 ① 08.00–20.00 Mon–Fri ⓝ Tram: 13, 15 to Môle

Só Mel £ ❹ Locals enjoy yummy Portuguese pastries at this unpretentious tea room. ⓐ 52 rue de Lausanne ① 022 732 34 58 ① 06.00–19.00 Thur–Tues ⓝ Tram: 13, 15 to Môle

AFTER DARK

RESTAURANTS

Café Gandhi £ ❺ Decorated with red velvet, woodcarvings and fairy lights, this unassuming restaurant serves tasty fish curries and dhal with fluffy naan breads. ⓐ 37 rue de Neuchâtel ❶ 022 731 61 61 ⓦ www.gandhi.ch ❶ 11.30–14.30, 19.00–24.00 Mon–Sat, 19.00–24.00 Sun Ⓝ Bus: 1 to Monthoux

Café de Paris £ ❻ Vegetarians beware! There's only one thing on the menu at this classic French bistro – steak served with fries. It can be a bit of a squeeze to get in, but the buzz adds to the atmosphere. ⓐ 26 rue du Mont-Blanc ❶ 022 732 84 50 ⓦ www.cafe-de-paris.ch ❶ 08.00–24.00 daily Ⓝ Bus: 8 to Mont-Blanc

Restaurant Mañana £ ❼ Feisty fajitas, vegetarian enchiladas and free-flowing tequila are on the menu at this Tex-Mex restaurant above the Cactus Club. ⓐ 3 rue Chaponnière, off rue des Alpes ❶ 022 732 21 31 ⓦ www.manana.ch ❶ 12.00–14.30, 18.00–23.30 daily Ⓝ Bus: 8 to Mont-Blanc

Ze do Pipo £ ❽ Tuck into *bacalhau assado* (baked cod) at this inviting little restaurant dishing up authentic Portuguese specialities. ⓐ 57 rue de Lausanne ❶ 022 738 88 21 ❶ 08.00–23.30 Mon–Sat Ⓝ Tram: 13, 15 to Môle

Edelweis £–££ ❾ With its rustic-kitsch décor, this lively, fun chalet-style restaurant brings the Alps to the heart of Geneva, with its traditional Swiss cuisine in hearty quantities and live music and yodelling nightly. ⓐ Place de la Navigation, off rue de Berne ⓣ 022 544 51 51 ⓛ 19.00–23.00 daily ⓝ Tram: 13, 14, or Bus 1 to place de la Navigation

Bistrot du Boeuf Rouge ££ ⑩ In the heart of the trendy Pâquis district, this bistro is a blast from the past. The menu specialises in Lyonnaise fare such as *andouillette beaujolaise* (tripe sausage) and *boudin noir* (blood sausage). ⓐ 17 rue Alfred-Vincent ⓣ 022 732 75 37 ⓦ www.boeufrouge.ch ⓛ 12.00–14.00, 19.00–22.00 Mon–Fri ⓝ Bus: 1 to Monthoux

El Mektoub ££ ⑪ You'd be forgiven for thinking you were in Marrakesh at this Aladdin's cave of a restaurant. Sample North African favourites like couscous and tender lamb with artichokes. ⓐ 5 rue Chaponnière, off rue des Alpes ⓣ 022 738 70 31 ⓛ 12.00–24.00 Mon–Fri, 18.00–24.00 Sat ⓝ Bus: 8 to Mont-Blanc

Le Chat-Botté £££ ⑫ Exquisite gastronomic dining and fine wines for that special occasion prepared by top-notch Swiss chef Dominique Gauthier, within the de-luxe Hotel Beau Rivage. ⓐ 13 quai du Mont-Blanc ⓣ 022 716 66 66 ⓦ www.beau-rivage.ch ⓝ Tram: 13, 14, or Bus 1 to place de la Navigation

BARS & CLUBS
Cactus Club Bursting with young partygoers at the weekends, this is the place to dance the night away. ⓐ 3 rue Chaponnière, off rue des Alpes ⓣ 022 732 21 31 ⓦ www.manana.ch ⓛ 18.00–02.00 Fri & Sat, 18.00–01.00 Sun–Thur ⓝ Bus: 8 to Mont-Blanc

Gold & Platinum If you're painting the Right Bank red, you'll probably wind up at this ultra-hip club where, after persuading the doormen to let you in, you'll enjoy Geneva's mega-sophisticated parties. ⓐ 18 quai du Seujet ⓣ 022 738 90 91 ⓦ www.goldandplatinum.ch ⓛ 19.00–05.00 daily ⓝ Tram: 16 to Isaac-Mercier

Java Club A trendy dance club in the basement of Geneva's top lakeside hotel, playing house and R'n'B sounds for a sleek, sophisticated crowd. ⓐ Grand Hotel Kempinski Geneva, 19 quai du Mont-Blanc ⓣ 022 908 90 88 ⓦ www.javaclub.ch ⓛ 23.00–05.00 Tues–Sat ⓝ Bus: 1 to Pâquis

Lord Jim This cheery British pub has some decent beers on tap and is a cosy spot to catch sports on the big screen. ⓐ 32 rue de Lausanne ⓣ 022 732 52 92 ⓦ www.lordjimpub.ch ⓛ 17.00–02.00 Mon–Sat ⓝ Tram: 13, 15 to Môle

Mr Pickwick Pub This cosy English pub claims to be Switzerland's oldest. Expect the works – from 13 beers on tap to big-screen sports, live bands, karaoke and quiz nights. ⓐ 80 rue de Lausanne ⓣ 022 731 67 97 ⓦ www.mrpickwick.ch ⓛ 10.00–02.00 daily ⓝ Tram: 13, 15 to Butini

Willi's This upbeat lounge bar is the place to see and be seen on the fashionable rue du Mont-Blanc. The terrace is perfect for people-watching. ⓐ 11 rue du Mont-Blanc ⓣ 022 732 77 09 ⓛ 07.00–02.00 Mon–Fri, 08.00–02.00 Sat, 09.00–02.00 Sun ⓝ Bus: 8 to Mont-Blanc

Carouge

Although just a 15-minute tram ride south of the centre, Carouge feels a world apart from Geneva. It was barely a speck on the map until 1754 when it became part of the Kingdom of Sardinia and King Victor Amédée III transformed the tiny hamlet into a flourishing town. The Piedmont landmarks that sprang up in the 18th century give the town its distinctly Italian atmosphere.

The beauty of Carouge lies in its understated charm and laid-back feel. While its sights might not quite rival those of other districts in Geneva, its sunny squares, pavement cafés and green-shuttered houses festooned with flower baskets ensure that it captivates nevertheless. You can easily spend a day here boutique-shopping, strolling the banks of the River Arve and soaking up the local flavour in bohemian cafés. This little taste of Sardinia is still off the beaten tourist track, so discover it soon.

SIGHTS & ATTRACTIONS

Église Ste-Croix (St Cross Church)

This Baroque cruciform church has a striking façade with slender columns, a central tower and Piedmontese elements – glance up to see the cockerel perching on the cross. An oasis of calm, the interior features grey-and-white frescoes, two rose windows and an organ dating from the Romantic period. But the church's greatest claim to fame is that it houses Switzerland's largest carillon, comprising 36 bells, which you're likely to hear before you see it. ⓐ Place du Marché ① 022 342 26 84 ⓦ www.sainte croix.ch ⓛ 09.00–18.30 daily ⓝ Tram: 12, 13 to Marché

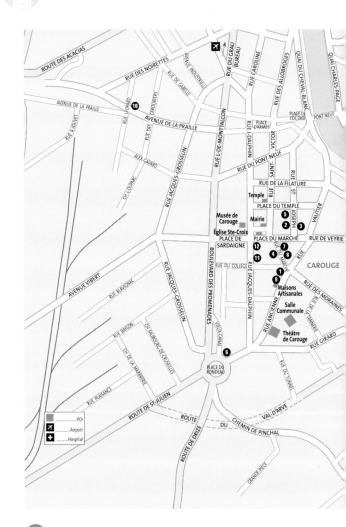

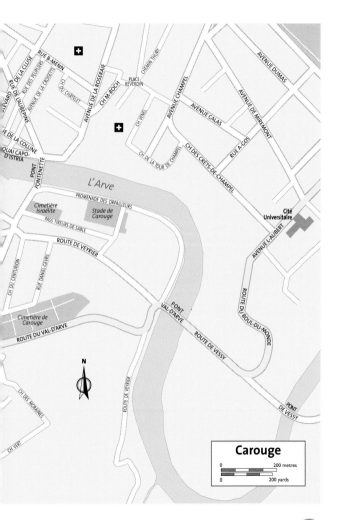

RUE DE LA CLUSE
RUE B-MENN
BOULEVARD DE L'AUBÉPINE
RUE DES PEUPLIERS
RUE DE L'AUBÉPINE
AVENUE DE LA CROISETTE
QU. CHÂTELET
AVENUE DE LA ROSERAIE
CH. M-ROCH
CHEMIN THURY
PLACE REVERDIN
AVENUE CHAMPEL
AVENUE CALAS
AVENUE DUMAS
AVENUE DE MIREMONT
CH. VINET
RUE DE LA COLLINE
QUAI CAPO D'ISTRIA
PONT FONTENETTE
CH. DE LA TOUR DE CHAMPEL
CH. DES CRÊTS-DE-CHAMPEL
RUE A-GOS

L'Arve

PROMENADE DES ORPAILLEURS

Cimetière Israélite
Stade de Carouge
PASS TIREURS-DE-SABLE

ROUTE DE VEYRIER

Cité Universitaire

AVENUE L-AUBERT

CH. DU CENTURION
RUE DANIEL-GEVRIL

Cimetière de Carouge
ROUTE DU VAL-D'ARVE

PONT VAL-D'ARVE
ROUTE DE VESSY

ROUTE DU BOUL-DU-MONDE

N

CH. DES MORAINES
CH. VERT
ROUTE DE VEYRIER

PONT DE VESSY

Carouge

0   200 metres
0   200 yards

Mairie (Town Hall)

Squatting in the shadow of the church, the Town Hall is the brainchild of Italian architect Giuseppe Piacenza. The sandy-coloured structure was built in 1777 as a presbytery and today it proudly flies the Carouge flag (a white lion beside a tree set against a red background). It is not open for visiting. ⓐ 14 place du Marché ⓦ www.carouge.ch ⓝ Tram: 12, 13 to Marché

Maisons Artisanales (Craftsmen's Houses)

Once home to the town's craftsmen, these Mediterranean-inspired houses are some of the best-preserved examples of 18th-century architecture in Carouge. Take a peek at their twisting staircases, arcades and leafy inner courtyards. ⓐ 8–30 rue Ancienne ⓝ Tram: 12, 13 to Marché

Place du Marché (Market Square)

The epicentre of Carouge life, this picture-perfect square is fringed with plane trees and overshadowed by the church. Be sure to look at the Blavignac fountain, a tribute to the River Arve shaped from rock and bronze. The twice-weekly market (see page 95) injects life into the square and a string of pavement cafés and restaurants reels in locals and visitors. It's a great spot to enjoy lunch or coffee and indulge in some prime people-watching. ⓝ Tram: 12, 13 to Marché

Pont-Neuf

With its trio of limestone arches, this bridge bears an uncanny resemblance to its namesake in Paris. Although the river has washed it away several times in the past, the current bridge, dating back to 1817, is built of sterner stuff. From here you can admire the silver-grey waters of the meandering River Arve, a tributary of the Rhône that's fed by Alpine glaciers. It's possible to stroll along the river's tree-lined banks and, if you're lucky, spot herons and beavers. ⊘ Tram: 12, 13 to Armes

Temple

Quite aptly named 'temple', this neoclassical church boasts peristyle columns and a Grecian-style pediment. Built in the early

▲ The elegant Église Ste-Croix

19th century, this gem includes Byzantine-style woodcarvings and elaborately frescoed vaults. It is open for guided tours and Sunday morning services only. ⓐ Place du Temple ⏱ Guided tours: 08.00–13.00 Wed & Sat Ⓝ Tram: 12, 13 to Marché

🔺 Take a tour of the neoclassical Temple

CULTURE

Musée de Carouge (Carouge Museum)

The imposing 18th-century Montanrouge House shelters this intriguing museum, which provides an insight into Carouge life past and present. Alongside temporary exhibitions, the permanent collection features a clutch of ceramics, paintings, Art Deco crafts and contemporary works by Carouge artists. Be sure to take a look at the Sardinian garden while you're there. ⓐ 2 place de Sardaigne ⓣ 022 342 33 83 ⓦ www.carouge.ch ⓛ 14.00–18.00 Tues–Sun ⓝ Tram: 12, 13 to Marché

Théâtre de Carouge (Carouge Theatre)

Experimental productions, cutting-edge plays and perennial favourites take to the stage of Carouge's intimate theatre, which was founded in 1958. ⓐ 57 rue Ancienne ⓣ 022 343 43 43 ⓦ www.tcag.ch ⓝ Tram: 13 to Carouge

RETAIL THERAPY

Auteur du Bain There is a whiff of nostalgia in this quirky shop, where tin tubs brim with dreamy bath products. Natural ingredients are used to create heart-shaped soaps on sticks and edible-looking bath sweets, cakes, chocolates, puddings and confetti. Lotions and potions scented with Moroccan rose, Egyptian jasmine and amber will make you want to run a bath straight away. ⓐ 12 rue St-Joseph ⓣ 022 300 52 73 ⓛ 10.30–18.30 Tues–Fri, 10.00–17.00 Sat, 12.00–16.00 Sun ⓝ Tram: 12, 13 to Marché

Betjeman & Barton The red walls are lined with every type of tea, teapot and cup imaginable at this cha-crazy store. A unique brew to look out for is *La Dame du Lac*, a blend of Mirabelle plum, strawberry, apple and caramel. You'll also find fresh ginger juice and lavender confiture here.

ⓐ 35 rue St-Joseph ⓣ 022 301 20 30 ⓦ www.barton.ch
ⓛ 09.45–17.30 Mon–Fri, 09.45–13.00, 14.00–17.00 Sat
ⓝ Tram: 12, 13 to Marché

CRAFTY CAROUGE

Carouge's creative roots stretch back to the 18th century, when the town was home to a plethora of carpenters, cobblers, blacksmiths, dressmakers, tanneries and watchmakers. The arty spirit is still alive and kicking today; the narrow streets a maze of musty antique shops, Lilliputian galleries and boutiques that are full of curiosities, original handicrafts and one-off local designs.

As you amble through the town, you'll come across the workshops and boutiques of potters, glass-blowers, ceramicists, jewellers, hatters, fashion designers, chocolatiers and confectioners. The beauty of shopping here is that you can often meet the makers themselves, and discover the raw materials and processes that go into their work. If you want high-street names and designer labels, stick to Geneva centre; but if you're seeking arty gifts, it has got to be crafty Carouge.

Bignens Vins This intoxicating store offers a staggering choice of regional and world wines. ⓐ 2 rue du Marché ⓣ 022 301 75 40 ⓦ www.bignens.ch ⓛ 08.30–12.30, 14.00–18.45 Mon–Sat ⓝ Tram: 12, 13 to Marché

Farmers' Market Taking over the main square twice a week, this market serves up voluptuous fruits, bunches of fresh lavender, farm-fresh Reblochon, handmade breads, truffles, home-made preserves and honey. Even if you don't plan to buy, come to soak up the buzzing atmosphere and taste local wines. ⓐ Place du Marché ⓛ 07.30–14.00 Wed & Sat ⓝ Tram: 12, 13 to Marché

Jean Kazès In this tiny watchmaker's atelier, Jean Kazès reinvents watchmaking with his wacky creations, which include clocks with magically suspended hands. ⓐ 21 rue St-Joseph ⓣ 022 343 30 92 ⓛ Phone ahead as hours vary ⓝ Tram: 12, 13 to Marché

Karavan Seray From mosaic vases to leatherwork and intricate woodcarvings, this shop stocks crafts from Tunisia, Morocco and Algeria. ⓐ 22 rue St-Joseph ⓣ 022 343 96 11 ⓛ 13.00–19.00 Mon–Fri, 09.30–17.00 Sat ⓝ Tram: 12, 13 to Marché

Michelle Dethurens The fine-quality craftsmanship and unusual creations by local potter Michelle Dethurens make unusual gift ideas. ⓐ 18 avenue Cardinal-Mermillod, off rue Vautier ⓣ 022 343 52 04 ⓛ Phone ahead as hours vary ⓝ Tram: 11, 12, 13 to Armes

Philippe Pascoët Master chocolatier Philippe Pascoët pours his passion and know-how into creating Carouge's finest chocolates.

The cocoa-rich pralines and truffles are infused with herbs like fresh mint, basil, star anis, rosemary, sage and even tobacco. 12 rue St-Joseph 022 301 20 58 www.philippe-pascoet.ch 13.00–18.00 Mon, 10.30–19.00 Tues–Fri, 10.00–17.30 Sat Tram: 12, 13 to Marché

Verrerie Bertin Artisanale It may look like marble or precious stones, but everything in this pocket-sized boutique is handcrafted from glass. 4 rue St-Joseph 022 343 10 43 15.00–18.30 Tues–Fri, 09.00–12.00 Sat Tram: 12, 13 to Marché

Zabo Hat lovers should visit this kooky boutique and workshop; it has colourful creations from the woolly to the wacky that will make you stand out from the crowd. 31 rue St-Joseph 022 301 75 76 www.zabo.ch 14.00–18.30 Tues, Wed & Fri, 12.00–16.00 Thur, 11.00–17.00 Sat Tram: 12, 13 to Marché

TAKING A BREAK

Calm £ ● It's easy to see the appeal of this effortlessly cool café: jazzy lounge music, delicious home-grown food and a relaxed vibe that will indeed leave you feeling very calm. Snacks include goat's-cheese quiche, yoghurt cake, warming soups and fresh-pressed juices. With wood beams, flickering candles and squishy leather chairs, the lounge is a great place to hibernate. 36 rue Ancienne 022 301 22 20 10.00–16.00 Tues, 10.00–18.00 Wed–Sun Tram: 13 to Carouge

Cupcakes & the City £ ❷ Treat yourself to a sweet treat at this delectable cakeshop, with its mouthwatering array of candy-coloured cupcakes. ⓐ 42 rue St-Joseph ⓣ 022 301 15 50 ⓦ www.cupcakesandthecity.ch ⓛ 09.00–19.00 Mon & Wed–Sat, 10.30–18.00 Sun ⓝ Tram: 12, 13 to Marché

Gelato Mania £ ❸ When the weather is warm, the handmade ice cream and sorbets at this hole-in-the-wall gelateria are refreshing. ⓐ 43 rue St-Joseph ⓣ 022 301 12 80 ⓛ 11.00–18.00 Tues–Sat (Mar–Apr); 11.00–24.00 daily (May–Oct) ⓝ Tram: 12, 13 to Marché

Martel £ ❹ Avid chocolate lovers should make for this *confiserie*, which serves mouthwatering pralines, éclairs and bite-sized petits fours. Sample them in the elegant tea room. ⓐ 8 rue du Marché ⓣ 022 342 00 45 ⓛ 07.30–19.00 Tues–Fri, 07.30–18.00 Sat & Sun ⓝ Tram: 12, 13 to Marché

Wolfisberg £ ❺ The smell of freshly baked bread fills the air at this spacious *pâtisserie* and tea room in the centre of town. The design is contemporary with bright colours, and the baguettes and pastries are superb. ⓐ 5 place du Temple ⓣ 022 342 32 19 ⓛ 06.30–19.00 daily ⓝ Tram: 12, 13 to Marché

AFTER DARK

RESTAURANTS
Au Boccalino £ ❻ Tiled floors and beamed ceilings give this cave-like restaurant the feel of a rustic Italian trattoria. The well-

prepared antipasti, wood-fired pizza and fresh salads served with Chianti would make mamma proud. **ⓐ** 4 place du Rondeau **ⓣ** 022 343 73 87 **ⓦ** www.restaurant-boccalino.ch **ⓛ** 11.30–14.30, 18.30–24.00 Mon–Thur, 11.30–14.30, 18.30–23.00 Fri & Sat, 11.30–15.00, 18.30–24.00 Sun **ⓝ** Tram: 13 to Carouge

La Bourse £ ❼ At the heart of Carouge, this classic brasserie is all exposed brick, warm wood and soft lighting. Pull up a chair in the frescoed cellar and choose between favourites such as *marmite du pêcheur* (fish casserole), champagne fondue and Bourgogne snails. The *prix-fixe* menu is chalked up on a blackboard. **ⓐ** 7 place du Marché **ⓣ** 022 342 04 66 **ⓦ** www.resto.ch/labourse **ⓛ** 12.00–14.00, 19.00–23.00 Tues–Sat **ⓝ** Tram: 12, 13 to Marché

Carlito £ ❽ The menu is predominantly Swiss at this snug wood-panelled bistro next to the church. The number of rösti potato specialities is staggering and the four-cheese fondue comes recommended. **ⓐ** 7 rue du Marché **ⓣ** 022 300 26 56 **ⓛ** 11.00–14.00, 18.00–22.00 daily **ⓝ** Tram: 12, 13 to Marché

Au Lion d'Or de Carouge £ ❾ Housed in a 300-year-old building, this unpretentious little restaurant draws locals who come for the flavoursome food and great-value *plat du jour*. Take a seat in the vaulted cellar or in the pretty courtyard to savour a fusion of French and Italian flavours with dishes such as risotto and duck foie gras with cider apples. **ⓐ** 53 rue Ancienne **ⓣ** 022 342 18 13 **ⓦ** www.lion-dor-carouge.ch **ⓛ** 12.00–13.30, 19.00–23.00 Mon–Fri, 19.00–23.00 Sat **ⓝ** Tram: 13 to Carouge

Le Babylone ££ ⑩ For all the splendour of a medieval banquet in a massive vaulted hall, tuck into such hearty fare as spit-roast chicken accompanied by jugglers and fire-eaters. ⓐ 40 avenue de la Praille ⓣ 022 343 14 00 ⓦ www.babylongeneve.com ⓛ 09.00–14.30, 18.30–02.00 Tues–Fri, 17.00–02.00 Sat

La Table ££ ⑪ Serious foodies are in for a treat at this stylish, light-filled restaurant close to the main square. It may look unassuming from outside, but it's the kitchen that counts. Dishes like curried salmon and tender lamb with ratatouille keep people coming back for more. ⓐ 31 rue Jacques-Dalphin ⓣ 022 301 13 22 ⓛ 16.00–02.00 Mon–Sat ⓜ Tram: 12, 13 to Marché

Au Vieux Carouge ££ ⑫ This classic Genevois restaurant is an old favourite with locals, unchanged over the years, and considered by many to serve the best cheese fondues in town. Booking is essential. ⓐ 27 rue Jacques-Dalphin ⓣ 022 342 64 98 ⓜ Tram: 12, 13 to Marché

BARS & CLUBS
Le Chat Noir If you want to get your claws into Carouge's after-dark scene, head for the Black Cat. Staging some of Geneva's hottest live music, the cellar of this hip venue resounds with everything from jazz to rock concerts, *chanson* and operetta. DJs on the decks keep the tiny dance floor crammed until the early hours of the morning. ⓐ 13 rue Vautier ⓣ 022 307 10 40 ⓦ www.chatnoir.ch ⓛ 18.00–04.00 Mon–Thur, 18.00–05.00 Fri & Sat ⓜ Tram: 12, 13 to Marché

L'Imprévu Black leather chairs, wood floors and original art make this a laid-back spot in which to enjoy a cappuccino by day or cocktail by night – try a mojito or Cuba libre. ⓐ 37–39 rue Vautier ⓣ 022 343 77 00 ⓛ 16.00–01.00 Tues–Thur, 16.00–02.00 Fri, 10.00–02.00 Sat, 17.00–24.00 Sun Ⓝ Tram: 12, 13 to Marché

Lion Rouge Pub This good old-fashioned pub is as far removed from 'posh' Geneva as they come. The cosy den is kitted out with a red telephone box and offers an arm-long list of beers including Amstel, Kilkenny and Erdinger. ⓐ 2 rue de Veyrier ⓣ 022 343 55 07 ⓛ 19.30–02.00 Mon–Sat Ⓝ Tram: 12, 13 to Marché

Qu'importe Inspired by Alfred de Musset's phrase '*Qu'importe le flacon ...*', this funky wine bar is a popular spot. Sink into the chocolate-hued leather sofas to unwind with a glass of wine and tapas by the fire. The terrace hums with life in summer. ⓐ 1 rue Ancienne ⓣ 022 342 15 25 ⓦ www.quimporte.ch ⓛ 17.00–24.00 Mon, 11.00–01.00 Tues–Thur, 11.00–02.00 Fri & Sat Ⓝ Tram: 12, 13 to Ancienne

---

ⓞ *Lausanne's impressive cathedral looms above the Old Town*

OUT OF TOWN
trips

Lausanne

Capital of the canton of Vaud, Lausanne is an effervescent university city that boasts pristine belle époque architecture, a hilltop medieval Old Town and a glut of vibrant bars.

GETTING THERE

The A1 motorway links Geneva to Lausanne and the journey takes 45 minutes by car. The city is also easy to reach by public transport, with SBB trains departing frequently from Geneva's main station with a journey time of approximately 45 minutes. Buses depart from Aéroport Genève-Cointrin (see page 48) roughly every 30 minutes from 08.00 to 20.00. In summer, a pleasant way to arrive is by ferry – contact **CGN** (ⓦ www.cgn.ch) for further details. The public transport details given in this chapter refer to bus and metro connections in Lausanne, not connections from Geneva to the city. Lausanne's metro, which opened in 2008, is the first metro in Switzerland.

SIGHTS & ATTRACTIONS

Cathédrale de Notre-Dame (Notre-Dame Cathedral)
Lausanne's Gothic cathedral looms large above the Old Town. Inside, light pierces the 13th-century rose window and imbues the interior with a sense of calm. For sweeping views over the city's rooftops, head for the terrace. ⓐ Place de la Cathédrale ⓣ 021 316 71 61 ⓛ 07.00–19.00 Mon–Fri, 08.00–19.00 Sat & Sun ⓜ Metro: Bessières

Château Saint-Maire (Saint-Maire Castle)

The spires of this 14th-century red-brick castle are like something out of a classic fairy tale. One-time home of bishops and Bernese bailiffs, it is now the seat of the cantonal government. The terrace affords far-reaching views over the city. ⓐ Place du Château ⏰ 10.00–19.00 Mon–Fri Ⓝ Bus: 16 to Pierre-Viret; 5, 6, 8 to Riponne

Hôtel de Ville (Town Hall)

The epicentre of Lausanne's Old Town, this arcaded Renaissance building overlooks the Fountain of Justice – get there on the hour to see historical figurines parade from the clock on the wall behind. It is not open for visiting. ⓐ Place de la Palud Ⓝ Metro: Riponne-Maurice-Béjart

🔺 Parade on the promenade at Ouchy

Geneva region

0 ——— 10 km
0 ——— 5 miles

La Chaux-du-Dombief
Pont-de-Poitte
Clairvaux-les-Lacs
Orgelet
JURA
Varennes-St-Sauveur
Cuiseaux
Chambéria
Charchilla
Lake Vouglans
Revermont
Sevron
A39
St-Amour
Arinthod
St-Claude
Coligny
St-Julien
Septmoncel
Ain
St-Étienne-du-Bois
Dortan
Les Bouchoux
Viry
Crêt de la Neige 1718 ▲
Revermont
Suran
Thoirette
Treffort-Cuisiat
Ain
Oyonnax
Semine
Viriat
Izernore
A404
Mont Burdet ▲ 1043
FRANCE
Péron
Bourg-en-Bresse
Le Grand Crêt d'Eau 1621 ▲
Valserine
Cevzériat
Nantua
St-Martin-du-Frêne
Collonges
A40
Lent
St-Martin-du-Mont
Châtillon-en-Michaille
Bellegarde-sur-Valserine
A40
AIN
Oignin
Ponein
Crêt des Éculaz 1014 ▲
Crêt du Nu 1351 ▲
Rhône
A42
Brénod
Jujurieux
Albarine
Frangy
Châtillon-la-Palud
Lyon
Ambronay
Ruffieu
Bassy
Germany
France
Switzerland
Geneva region
Italy
St-Rambert-en-Bugey
Seyssel
Thusy
Cluse des Hôpitaux
Séran
Fur
Champagne-en-Valromey
Grand Colombier 1531 ▲
Artemare
Rumilly
Villebois
Ruffieux

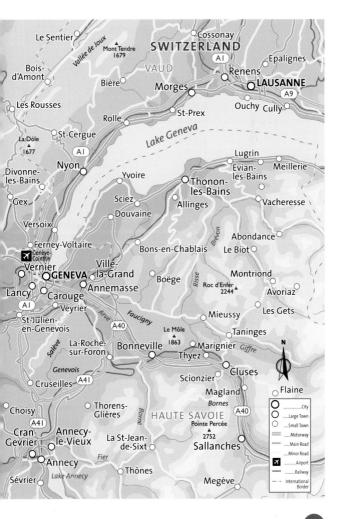

Jardin Botanique (Botanic Gardens)

Steep paths weave through these hilltop botanic gardens, which are home to 6,000 species, including medicinal, Alpine and tropical plants. From the top there are 360° views over Lausanne and the lake. ⓐ Avenue de Beauregard ⓣ 021 316 99 88 ⓦ www.botanique.vd.ch ⓛ 10.00–17.30 daily (Mar–Oct) ⓝ Bus: 1 to Beauregard

Ouchy

The port of Ouchy is a far cry from the city's bustle: the waterfront promenade is where the locals come to relax, stroll and drink in views of the Alps. Fringed with flower-strewn gardens, the quays are home to grand hotels, the Olympic Park and a castle. Boats bobbing in the marina and street entertainers give it a seaside feel. ⓐ Quai d'Ouchy ⓝ Metro: Ouchy; Bus: 2 to Navigation

CULTURE

Fondation de l'Hermitage

Situated in the Bois de Sauvabelin park, this pink 19th-century residence houses an exceptional permanent collection featuring works by Degas, Sisley and Magritte. The gallery frequently hosts temporary exhibitions too. ⓐ 2 route du Signal ⓣ 021 320 50 01 ⓦ www.fondation-hermitage.ch ⓛ 10.00–18.00 Tues–Sun ⓝ Bus: 3 to Motte ⓘ Admission charge

Musée Historique (History Museum)

This intriguing museum opposite the cathedral traces Lausanne's history from the Ice Age to the 20th century. Low-beamed rooms and narrow passageways are the backdrop for chronological displays that include Neolithic skeletons, religious iconography, silverware and antique musical instruments. ⓐ 4 place de la Cathédrale ⓣ 021 315 41 01 ⓦ www.lausanne.ch/mhl ⓛ 11.00–18.00 Tues–Thur, 11.00–17.00 Fri–Sun ⓜ Metro: Bessières; Bus: 16 to Pierre-Viret ⓘ Admission charge

Musée Olympique (Olympic Museum)
Shaped from marble and soaring above the Olympic Park on Ouchy embankment, this monumental building is a tribute to Lausanne's Olympic heritage – the city has been home to the International Olympic Committee (IOC) since 1915. Themed displays cover all aspects of the Games. ⓐ Quai d'Ouchy ⓣ 021 621 65 11 ⓦ www.olympic.org ⓛ 09.00–18.00 daily (Apr–Oct); 09.00–18.00 Tues–Sun (Nov–Mar) ⓜ Bus: 8 to Musée Olympique ⓘ Admission charge

Opéra de Lausanne (Lausanne Opera)
The acclaimed Lausanne Opera presents an eclectic repertoire of opera, dance, classical concerts and recitals. The season runs from October to May. ⓐ 12 avenue du Théâtre ⓣ 021 310 16 16; Box office: 021 310 16 00 ⓦ www.opera-lausanne.ch ⓛ 09.00–18.30 daily ⓜ Bus: 9, 12 to Georgette

Palais de Rumine (Rumine Palace)
The sheer scale of this neo-Renaissance building towering above place de la Riponne is impressive. The ornate façade shelters a clutch of fascinating museums, including the Fine Arts Museum, the Archaeology & History Museum and the

Zoological Museum. Highlights include the reconstruction of a Neolithic cave and masterpieces by Swiss artist Charles Gleyre. ⓐ 6 place de la Riponne ⓣ 021 692 44 70 ⓛ 11.00–18.00 Tues & Wed, 11.00–20.00 Thur, 11.00–17.00 Fri–Sun ⓝ Metro: Riponne-Maurice-Béjart; Bus: 5, 6, 8 to Riponne ❶ Admission charge

RETAIL THERAPY

Art Suisse Contemporary creations by Swiss artists are the big draw here. ⓐ 1 place du Port ⓣ 021 320 81 80 ⓛ 12.30–18.15 Tues–Fri, 09.30–17.00 Sat ⓝ Metro: Ouchy

Durig Cocoa-mad Dan Durig creates divine sweets including Venezuelan milk truffles and organic chocolate plums.
ⓐ 15 avenue d'Ouchy ⓣ 021 601 24 35 ⓦ www.durig.ch
ⓛ 08.30–18.30 Tues–Fri, 08.30–17.00 Sat
ⓝ Bus: 2 to Closelet

La Ferme Vaudoise This store is well stocked with Vaud specialities, from Mont d'Or cheese to handmade sausages.
ⓐ 5 place de la Palud ⓣ 021 351 35 55 ⓛ 09.00–13.00, 14.00–18.30 Mon–Fri, 07.30–17.00 Sat ⓝ Bus: 16 to Pierre-Viret

L'Herboriste This old-world shop is crammed with herbal teas, remedies, natural cosmetics, fragrances and essential oils.
ⓐ 12 avenue du Léman ⓣ 021 311 81 70 ⓦ www.lherboriste.ch
ⓛ 14.00–18.30 Mon, 08.30–12.30, 14.00–18.30 Tues–Fri, 08.30–17.00 Sat ⓝ Bus: 9 to avenue du Léman

TheTeaTee Around 160 blends of tea and delicate china line the walls of this inviting shop. 4 rue Enning 021 312 48 63 www.theteatee.ch 13.30–18.30 Mon, 09.30–18.30 Tues–Fri, 09.30–17.00 Sat Bus: 17 to Benjamin-Constant

TAKING A BREAK

Délices du Chocolat £ Smart tea room serving luscious apple tarts, petits fours and pastries. 2–4 rue Enning 021 320 24 24 07.00–19.00 Mon–Fri, 07.00–18.00 Sat, 07.00–13.00 Sun Bus: 17 to Benjamin-Constant

● The magnificent Palais de Rumine

L'Éléphant Blanc £ This charming restaurant's menu is limited but superbly cooked, from duck foie gras to crème brûlée. ⓐ 4 rue Cité-Devant ⓣ 021 312 64 89 ⓦ www.lelephantblanc.ch ⓛ 11.30–14.30, 18.30–24.00 Tues–Sat ⓝ Bus: 16 to Pierre-Viret

Fox Café £ This spacious New York-style diner serves up tasty omelettes, curries, pasta dishes and mussels. ⓐ 10 rue Enning ⓣ 021 323 32 18 ⓛ 07.30–01.00 Mon–Thur, 07.30–02.00 Fri & Sat, 17.00–01.00 Sun ⓝ Bus: 17 to Benjamin-Constant

AFTER DARK

RESTAURANTS
Café du Grütli £ Enjoy simple homely cuisine including cheese platters and the local *papet vaudois* speciality – sausage and leek casserole. ⓐ 4 rue de la Mercerie ⓣ 021 312 94 93

⬥ *Specially for the sweet-toothed: Délices du Chocolat*

🌐 www.cafedugruetli.ch 🕐 09.00–14.30, 18.30–23.30 Mon, Tues, Thur & Fri, 08.30–14.30, 18.30–23.30 Wed, 08.30–15.30, 18.30–23.30 Sat Ⓝ Bus: 16 to Pierre-Viret

Café Romand £ Enjoy cheese fondue at this elegant Swiss brasserie. ⓐ 2 place St-François ☎ 021 312 63 75 🌐 www.caferomand.com 🕐 09.00–01.00 Mon–Sat Ⓝ Bus: 2, 4, 8 to St-François

Au Couscous £ This hole-in-the-wall restaurant is a well-kept secret. Savour Lebanese meze, merguez and sticky baklava. ⓐ 2 rue Enning ☎ 021 321 98 00 🌐 www.au-couscous.ch 🕐 11.30–14.00, 18.30–01.30 Mon–Sat, 18.30–01.30 Sun Ⓝ Bus: 17 to Benjamin-Constant

Le Java £ This galleried restaurant fuses arabesque touches with Art Deco nostalgia. The menu is equally inspired. ⓐ 36 rue Marterey ☎ 021 321 38 37 🌐 www.lejava.ch 🕐 07.00–24.00 Mon–Wed, 07.00–01.00 Thur & Fri, 09.30–01.00 Sat, 09.30–24.00 Sun Ⓝ Bus: 17 to Benjamin-Constant

Le Pirate ££ Delicious fish from the lake is the speciality of this jolly lakeside restaurant in Ouchy. ⓐ 4 place de la Navigation ☎ 021 613 15 00 🌐 www.aulac.ch 🕐 10.00–24.00 daily Ⓝ Metro: Ouchy

Beau Rivage £££ One of the most prestigious hotels on Lake Geneva, renowned for its fine service, gourmet cuisine, world-class spa, and its setting – within a beautiful neo-Baroque palace on the lake edge with a magnificent Alpine backdrop. ⓐ 6 Lausanne-Ouchy ☎ 021 613 33 33 🌐 www.brp.ch Ⓝ Metro: Ouchy

BARS & CLUBS

Bleu Lézard One of Lausanne's hippest haunts, this upbeat bar draws a lively crowd. ⓐ 10 rue Enning ① 021 321 38 30 Ⓦ www.bleu-lezard.ch ① 07.00–01.00 Mon–Thur, 07.00–02.00 Fri, 08.00–02.00 Sat, 09.30–01.00 Sun Ⓝ Bus: 17 to Benjamin-Constant

Les Brasseurs Copper vats and wood floors make this micro-brewery an inviting place to enjoy a beer and some sauerkraut. ⓐ 4 rue Centrale ① 021 351 14 24 Ⓦ www.les-brasseurs.ch ① 11.00–01.00 Mon–Thur, 11.00–02.00 Fri & Sat, 16.00–24.00 Sun Ⓝ Bus: 2 to Bel-Air

Captain Cook Pub This cheery English pub serves real ales and bar food and shows big-screen sports. ⓐ 2 rue Enning ① 021 323 00 55 Ⓦ www.captain-cook.ch ① 16.00–01.00 Mon–Thur, 16.00–02.00 Fri & Sat, 17.00–24.00 Sun Ⓝ Bus: 17 to Benjamin-Constant

D! Club Party till dawn to live acts and electro-house music at this funky club. ⓐ 15 place Centrale ① 021 351 51 40 Ⓦ www.dclub.ch ① 21.00–02.00 Wed, 21.00–04.00 Thur, 21.00–05.00 Fri & Sat Ⓝ Bus: 2 to Bel-Air

Le Lounge Part of Ouchy's medieval château, this lounge-style bar affords uninterrupted views of the lake through floor-to-ceiling glass windows. ⓐ 2 place du Port ① 021 331 32 32 Ⓦ www.chateaudouchy.ch ① 10.00–01.00 Mon–Thur, 10.00–02.00 Fri & Sat, 16.00–24.00 Sun Ⓝ Metro: Ouchy; Bus: 2 to Ouchy

ACCOMMODATION

Camping de Vidy £ A stone's throw from Ouchy, this lake-front campsite is open year-round, with a supermarket, play area, laundry and restaurant. 🅐 3 chemin du Camping 🕿 021 622 50 00 🌐 www.campinglausannevidy.ch 🕒 Apr–Oct 🚍 Bus: 2 to Bois de Vaux

Lausanne YH £ Set in attractive grounds by the lake and open all year, this hostel features clean and bright singles, doubles and dorms. 🅐 36 chemin du Bois-de-Vaux 🕿 021 626 02 22 🌐 www.youthhostel.ch/lausanne 🚍 Bus: 2 to Bois de Vaux

Hôtel Élite ££ Surrounded by gardens, this stylish hotel is one of Lausanne's best mid-range options. Choose the top floor for lake views. 🅐 1 avenue Sainte-Luce 🕿 021 320 23 61 🌐 www.elite-lausanne.ch 🚍 Bus: 2, 4, 8 to St-François

VINE TIME

At the heart of vine-clad Vaud, the precipitous terraces surrounding Lausanne are prime wine-growing territory. A great way to explore them is to don walking boots or hire a bicycle, pausing in the cellars en route. The 33-km (21-mile) Lavaux Wine Trail from Ouchy to Chillon passes through such vintners' villages as Lutry, Riex and Chardonne and will give you intoxicating lake and Alpine views.

Annecy

Situated on the northern tip of turquoise Lake Annecy, it's easy to see Annecy's appeal: pure Alpine waters framed by jagged peaks, flower-lined canals and a medieval castle overshadowing the Old Town's warren of cobbled streets. Life here is laid-back, and simple pleasures like savouring fresh lake trout or strolling on waterfront promenades are a delight. For those seeking more adventure, Annecy's big and beautiful backyard provides a range of outdoor action including kayaking, climbing and skiing in the nearby Alps.

GETTING THERE

The speedy A41 motorway links Geneva to Annecy in just 40 minutes. The French town is also accessible by public transport, with SNCF trains operating a frequent service to Annecy's main station. **Sibra buses** (ⓦ www.sibra.fr) serve the town and surrounding villages. The public transport details given in this chapter refer to connections in Annecy, not connections from Geneva to the city.

SIGHTS & ATTRACTIONS

Basilique de la Visitation

On top of a wooded hill, this early 20th-century basilica features a striking 72-m (236-ft) steeple and offers sweeping views over Annecy. ⓐ Avenue de la Visitation ⓣ 04 50 45 20 30 ⓛ 07.00–12.00, 14.00–19.00 daily ⓝ Bus: 14 to Visitation

The turquoise tranquillity of Lake Annecy

● *From town gaol to tourist delight: Palais de l'Île*

Château d'Annecy (Annecy Castle)

Set against a backdrop of snow-capped mountains, this red-turreted castle looms large above Annecy. Sturdy towers soar above the cobbled inner courtyard, the oldest dating back to the 13th century. From this fairy-tale perch, you can enjoy superb views of the lake and town. ⓐ Place du Château ⓣ 04 50 33 87 30 ⓞ 10.30–18.00 daily (June–Sept); 10.00–12.00, 14.00–17.00 Wed–Mon (Oct–May) ⓝ Bus: 7, 14 to Paradis

Jardins de l'Europe

Locals hang out by the lake's edge in these pristine gardens, which have plenty of shady nooks in which to relax and watch the world go by. Enjoy a picnic beneath the trees, stroll to Lovers' Bridge and glimpse the tiny Île des Cygnes (Swan Island). ⓐ Quai Napoleon III ⓝ Bus: 6, 7, 15 to Hôtel de Ville

Palais de l'Île

Annecy's picture-perfect landmark belies its function as the town's former prison. With its wistful turrets rising high above the Thiou Canal, this medieval icon is one of France's most photographed buildings. Step inside to explore a labyrinth of cells and wander the banks to watch local artists at work. ⓐ 3 passage de l'Île ⓣ 04 50 33 87 30 ⓞ 10.30–18.00 daily (June–Sept); 10.00–12.00, 14.00–17.00 Wed–Mon (Oct–May) ⓝ Bus: 6, 7, 15 to Hôtel de Ville ⓘ Admission charge

Pont des Amours (Lovers' Bridge)

Straddling the Vassé Canal, this arched bridge links the Jardins de l'Europe to Champs de Mars promenade. Romantic couples

come here to walk hand in hand; singletons can fall in love with the views of Lake Annecy instead. Champs de Mars Bus: 6, 7, 15 to Hôtel de Ville

CULTURE

Musée Château d'Annecy (Annecy Castle Museum)
Housed in the castle, this museum traces Annecy's intriguing history, with its displays of traditional Savoy furniture, contemporary art and Alpine anthropology. Place du Château 04 50 33 87 30 musees@anglo-annecy.fr 10.30–18.00 daily (June–Sept); 10.00–12.00, 14.00–17.00 Wed–Mon (Oct–May) Bus: 7, 14 to Paradis Admission charge

RECREATION

Annecy Aventure This sports centre organises a wide range of recreational activities including dog-sledding, snow shoeing, ski touring and even ice-climbing in the winter. Or test your skills at paragliding, rafting, canyoning and Via Ferrata in summer, as

KING OF 12 CASTLES …

Passing through Annecy, the Road of the Dukes of Savoy links 12 historic castles, abbeys and forts, from the Castle of Menthon-Saint-Bernard to the Castle of Chambéry. As well as tracing the region's fascinating heritage, the route takes in some spectacular Alpine scenery. www.chateaux-france.com/route-savoie

◆ *The Château d'Annecy houses the Castle Museum*

well as hiring out mountain bikes and sailing boats. 🅐 9 rue du Bel Air ☏ 04 50 45 38 46 🆆 www.annecy-aventure.com 🕒 09.00–19.00 daily

Bateaux Dupraz A mini-cruise is a relaxed way to tour the lake and see the sights. Boats with guided commentary depart regularly in summer. 🅐 Jardins de l'Europe ☏ 04 50 52 42 99 🆆 www.bateauxdupraz.com 🕒 11.45, 13.15, 14.30, 15.45, 17.15, 18.30 daily (Apr–mid-Nov) 🚍 Bus: 6, 7, 15 to Hôtel de Ville

Gorges du Fier A 15-minute journey from Annecy, Lovagny boasts one of France's most dramatic river gorges. This precipitous ravine's bizarre rock formations and high footbridges are very impressive. 🅐 Lovagny ☏ 04 50 46 23 07 🆆 www.gorgesdufier.com 🕒 09.30–18.15 (mid-Mar–mid-June & mid-Sept–mid-Oct), last entry 17.15; 09.30–19.15 (mid-June–mid-Sept), last entry 18.15 🚍 Bus: 62 to Lovagny ❶ Admission charge

Marquisats Swimming Pool & Beach With its trio of outdoor pools, this lido by the lake is the ideal spot to swim and relax in summer. 🅐 29 rue des Marquisats ☏ 04 50 33 65 40 🕒 10.00–19.00 daily (May–Sept) 🚍 Bus: 6 to Hôpital Marquisats ❶ Admission charge

Takamaka Adrenalin junkies enjoy activities like canyoning, sky diving, downhill mountain biking and paragliding at this extreme sports centre. 🅐 23 Faubourg Sainte-Claire ☏ 04 50 45 60 61 🆆 www.takamaka.fr 🕒 09.00–19.00 daily (Apr–Oct) 🚍 Bus: 4, 7 to Fauré

RETAIL THERAPY

Courier This modern shopping mall shelters 40 high-street stores under its glass roof, including names like H&M, Fnac and Sephora. ⓐ 65 rue Carnot ⓣ 04 50 46 46 76 ⓦ www.centre-courier.com ⓛ 09.30–19.30 Mon–Sat ⓝ Bus: 2, 3, 6, 9, 10, 14 to Courier

Crèmerie du Lac Fans of *fromage* sniff out Alain Michel's store, crammed with different cheeses. Look out for Savoy classics like flavoursome Reblochon and Roquefort ripened in a cool cellar. ⓐ 3 rue du Lac ⓣ 04 50 45 19 31 ⓦ www.cremeriedulac.com ⓛ 07.30–12.15, 15.00–19.15 Tues–Sat ⓝ Bus: 6, 7, 15 to Hôtel de Ville

Farmers' Market Potter around Annecy's vibrant market, where stalls are piled high with local produce, from wheels of Savoy cheese to fresh fruit, plump olives, sausages and handmade bread. ⓐ Rue de la République, rue Sainte-Claire, Pont-Morens ⓛ 08.00–12.00 Tues, Fri & Sun ⓝ Bus: 6, 7, 15 to Hôtel de Ville

TAKING A BREAK

Au Fidèle Berger £ It's hard to resist *les cloches d'Annecy* (bells of Annecy) pralines here, where the scent of hot chocolate fills the air. If you're sweet enough already, try one of the speciality teas. ⓐ 2 rue Royale ⓣ 04 50 45 00 32 ⓛ 09.15–19.00 Tues–Fri, 09.00–19.30 Sat ⓝ Bus: 6, 7, 15 to Hôtel de Ville

Nature et Saveur £ This restaurant only uses the freshest local produce to create imaginative vegetarian options, delicious

fresh salads and even healthy (!) desserts. ⓐ Place des Cordeliers
ⓣ 04 50 45 82 29 ⓦ www.nature-saveur.com ⓛ 08.30–19.00
Tues–Sat ⓝ Bus: 6, 7, 15 to Hôtel de Ville

Passion Gourmande £ If you're crazy about crêpes, this central
café is for you. The lunch menu offers great value and there
is a sunny terrace. ⓐ 16 rue Sainte-Claire ⓣ 04 50 52 92 78
ⓛ 12.00–14.00, 19.00–23.00 daily ⓝ Bus: 6, 7, 15 to Hôtel de Ville

AFTER DARK

RESTAURANTS

Le Lilas Rose £ When it's cold outside, this canal-side bistro
dishes up hearty Savoyard Alpine fare like raclette, gooey
fondue and tartiflettes. ⓐ Passage de l'Évêché ⓣ 04 50 45 37 08
ⓛ 12.00–14.00, 19.00–23.00 daily ⓝ Bus: 6, 7, 15 to Hôtel de Ville

Le Munich £ This lively brasserie and bar overlooks the Thiou
Canal. Munch on sauerkraut with sausage, knuckle of ham or
mussels and chips. There are 13 draught beers to choose from.
ⓐ 1 quai Perrière ⓣ 04 50 45 02 11 ⓦ www.lemunich.com
ⓛ 08.00–02.00 daily ⓝ Bus: 6, 7, 15 to Hôtel de Ville

Super Panorama £ The name of this restaurant says it all: the
lake and mountain views from the terrace are as appetising
as the cuisine. Try the trout with almonds with a glass of
crisp Apremont. ⓐ 7 route du Semnoz ⓣ 04 50 45 34 86
ⓦ www.super-panorama.fr ⓛ 12.00–16.00 Mon,
12.00–22.00 Wed–Sun ⓝ Bus: 6 to Hôtel de Police

Auberge de Savoie ££ Fish doesn't come fresher than at this gourmet haunt, located on an attractive square opposite the Palais de l'Île. ⓐ 1 place St-François de Sales ⓣ 04 50 45 03 05 ⓦ www.aubergedesavoie.fr ⓛ 12.00–14.00, 19.30–22.00 Thur–Mon ⓝ Bus: 6, 7, 15 to Hôtel de Ville

La Ciboulette ££–£££ Georges Paccard cooks up a storm at this gem of a restaurant. Specialities include Pauillac lamb and filet of turbot, all served on the terrace. ⓐ 10 rue Vaugelas ⓣ 04 50 45 74 57 ⓦ www.laciboulette-annecy.com ⓛ 12.00–14.00, 19.30–23.00 Tues–Sat ⓝ Bus: 6, 7, 15 to Hôtel de Ville

BARS & CLUBS
Le Fauteuil Paresseux A favourite among Annecy's student population, this stylish candlelit bar is a lively venue for happy-hour cocktails, followed by DJs playing an eclectic mix from electro to chart toppers. ⓐ 6 rue Vaugelas ⓣ 04 50 51 69 39 ⓛ 12.00–01.00 Mon–Sat

Red'z Partygoers head for this hip club in the heart of Annecy, where DJs spin techno and house. ⓐ 14 rue Perrière ⓣ 06 21 72 77 22 ⓛ 11.00–03.00 daily (Apr–Sept); 15.30–03.00 daily (Oct–Mar) ⓝ Bus: 6, 7, 15 to Hôtel de Ville

ACCOMMODATION

Auberge de Jeunesse Annecy £ A brisk uphill hike takes you to this cheery lodge-style hostel, bordering the forest and affording superb views. It has a snug bar, spotless dorms and

provides good-value meals. ⓐ 4 route du Semnoz ⓣ 04 50 45 33 19
ⓦ www.auberge-annecy.com/fr ⓛ Apr–Oct ⓝ Bus: 6 to Hôtel
de Police

Camping Le Belvédère £ This is close enough to the lake for
a dip before breakfast, only ten minutes from the beach and the
Old Town. On-site facilities at this green and tranquil location
include a laundry, mini-market and playground. ⓐ 8 route du
Semnoz ⓣ 04 50 45 48 30 ⓔ camping@ville-annecy.fr ⓛ Apr–Oct
ⓝ Bus: 6 to Hôtel de Police

Hôtel du Château £ Nestled at the foot of the castle, this family-
run hotel has an intimate feel. Rooms are simple but comfortable
and offer fine views. ⓐ 16 rampe du Château ⓣ 04 50 45 27 66
ⓦ www.annecy-hotel.com ⓝ Bus: 7, 14 to Paradis

Hôtel du Nord £ Close to the lake, this peaceful hotel is an ideal
base. The rooms are decorated in warm hues and feature modern
bathrooms. There is free parking and a generous breakfast buffet.
ⓐ 24 rue Sommeiller ⓣ 04 50 45 08 78 ⓦ www.annecy-hotel-du-
nord.com ⓝ Bus: 6, 7, 15 to Hôtel de Ville

ⓞ *Geneva's riverside tourist office*

PRACTICAL
information

Directory

GETTING THERE

By air

Many airlines operate a frequent, direct service between Genève-Cointrin International Airport (see page 48) and around 90 destinations including London, New York, Paris and Rome. Baboo, easyJet and bmibaby offer some of the best budget flights. Other key airlines include British Airways, Continental Airlines, Swiss and KLM.

Baboo ⓦ www.flybaboo.com

bmibaby ⓦ www.bmibaby.com

British Airways ⓦ www.britishairways.com

Continental Airlines ⓦ www.continental.com

easyJet ⓦ www.easyjet.com

KLM ⓦ www.klm.com

Swiss ⓦ www.swiss.com

Many people are aware that air travel emits CO_2, which contributes to climate change. You may be interested in the possibility of lessening the environmental impact of your flight through the charity **Climate Care** (ⓦ www.jpmorganclimate care.com), which offsets your CO_2 by funding environmental projects around the world.

By rail

Geneva's main station, Gare de Cornavin, has excellent connections on high-speed trains to major Swiss cities including Lausanne, Bern, Basel and Zurich, as well as serving European cities including Lyon, Paris, Barcelona and Venice. Swiss Federal

Railways provides detailed information on routes and timetables.
SBB ☎ 0900 300 300 🌐 www.sbb.ch

The monthly *Thomas Cook European Rail Timetable* has up-to-date
schedules for European international and national train services.
Thomas Cook European Rail Timetable ☎ (UK) 01733 416477;
(USA) 1 800 322 3834 🌐 www.thomascookpublishing.com

By road

International and long-distance buses depart from Geneva's main
bus station on place Dorcière, operating to destinations including
Lyon, Rome and London. For details of bus services in and around
Geneva see 🌐 www.tpg.ch. **Eurolines** (🌐 www.eurolines.com)
also offers international bus services to the city.

🔺 *An SNCF train pulls into Gare de Cornavin, the central railway station*

Switzerland's roads are well maintained, driving is on the right and international signs are used. The speed limit is strictly enforced, with cameras operating on most stretches of motorway and speeding offences often subject to hefty on-the-spot fines. To drive on Switzerland's motorways, you'll need to purchase a *Vignette* (toll sticker) to display in the front windscreen. On a clear run, you can reach Lausanne in 45 minutes, Lyon in 1 hour 30 minutes and Zurich in 2 hours 30 minutes.

ENTRY FORMALITIES

EU, Australian, Canadian, New Zealand, South African and United States citizens must have a valid passport to enter Switzerland, but do not require a visa for stays of fewer than 90 days. If you are arriving from countries other than these, you may need a visa and should contact your consulate or embassy up to three months before departure. The **Swiss Federal Department of Foreign Affairs** (ⓦ www.eda.admin.ch) provides more information on entry requirements.

It is usually free to import goods from a non-EU country, but you should check restrictions on the imports of tobacco, perfume and alcohol. Further information is available at ⓦ www.ezv.admin.ch

MONEY

Switzerland's currency is the Swiss franc (CHF), divided up into 100 rappen or centimes. Coins are in denominations of CHF5, 2 and 1, and 50, 20, 10 and 5 centimes. There are banknotes of 10, 20, 50, 100, 200 and 1,000 francs. Some of Geneva's restaurants, hotels and shops also accept euros, but remember that you will be given the change back in Swiss francs.

Central Geneva has plenty of ATMs where you can withdraw cash with your credit or debit card 24 hours a day, although it's worth checking whether the bank imposes a fee.

There are bureaux de change in banks, the main train station and the airport. Traveller's cheques can be cashed in most bureaux de change, banks, travel agencies and hotels. Banks generally offer the best rates. Visa, MasterCard, Diners Club and American Express are widely accepted.

HEALTH, SAFETY & CRIME

Geneva is a clean and safe city to visit, and there are no particular health risks. No immunisations or health certificates are required and the tap water is safe to drink.

While Switzerland has one of the best standards of medical care in the world, treatment can be expensive, so it's wise to invest in a good health insurance policy before visiting. EU citizens are entitled to free or reduced-cost emergency healthcare with a valid European Health Insurance Card (EHIC), which entitles you to state medical treatment but does not cover repatriation or long-term illness.

Pharmacies can treat minor ailments and are usually open 07.45–18.30 Monday to Friday and 08.00–17.00 Saturday. The **Geneva Pharmacies Association** (Ⓦ www.pharmacies-geneve.ch) lists 24-hour pharmacies on its website. Your hotel should be able to arrange for you to see an English-speaking doctor, if necessary.

The crime rate in Geneva is low, so you shouldn't experience any problems during your stay. However, pickpockets may operate in key tourist areas, so it's wise to keep an eye on your possessions. If you are the victim of a crime, you should inform the police by calling 117 (see *Emergencies*, page 136).

OPENING HOURS

Banks open 08.30–16.30 Monday to Friday. All close at weekends, but many have 24-hour ATMs.

Most shops open 09.00–19.00 Monday to Saturday; smaller boutiques often close for lunch. Some shopping malls and department stores stay open until 21.00 on Thursdays.

TOILETS

There are clean public toilets in the centre of Geneva, with most offering baby-changing facilities and access to disabled travellers. You'll need 50 centimes to use the city's automatic, self-cleaning toilets. Most cafés, restaurants and some department stores have free toilets for customers.

CHILDREN

Extremely clean and easy to negotiate, this family-friendly city has a range of attractions to keep children amused. There is often a 50 per cent reduction for children, and kids are welcome in most restaurants and cafés.

Bains des Pâquis The Right Bank's pier is a relaxed spot for families to enjoy a picnic and swim (see page 74).

Bois de la Bâtie (Bâtie Woods) Children will love to explore the caves, gorges and woodlands. There's also a splash pool and playground. ⓐ Bâtie ⓝ Bus: 2, 11 to Bâtie

🔺 *There's plenty of fun for kids*

GENEVA PASS

Families can save by purchasing a Geneva Card, offering free access to the public transport network and entry to many top museums and attractions, plus reductions in some boat trips, tours, shops and restaurants. The card is available for one, two or three days and can be purchased from the tourist information centre (see page 135).

Genève-Plage (Geneva Beach) Tots enjoy the paddling pool, sandpit and slides here, while teens head for the Olympic Swimming Pool, diving boards and volleyball court (see page 33).

Mini-train In summer, a mini-train chugs through Geneva's streets to take in the key sights. ⓐ Rotonde du Mont-Blanc ⓣ 022 781 04 04 ⓦ www.sttr.ch ⓛ 10.00–dusk daily (Mar–Oct) ⓝ Bus: 8 to Chantepoulet

Vivarium Lausanne Children can spot crocodiles, turtles, anacondas and lizards at one of Europe's leading vivariums. ⓐ 82 chemin de Boissonnet, Lausanne ⓣ 021 652 72 94 ⓦ www.vivarium-lausanne.ch ⓛ 13.00–18.00 Mon & Fri, 10.00–18.00 Wed, Sat & Sun, 13.00–22.00 Thur ⓝ Bus: 16 to Vivarium ⓘ Admission charge

COMMUNICATION
Internet

Wireless Internet access (Wi-Fi) has become widespread in Geneva with many cafés, restaurants, bars, hotels and even petrol stations offering the service. The following website gives details on free hotspots in Switzerland: Ⓦ www.freespot.ch

There is a handful of Internet cafés in the centre of Geneva that offer a high-speed broadband connection. Expect to pay between CHF5 and CHF10 for an hour online.

Charly's Check Point Offers Internet access as well as services like scanning and faxing. ⓐ 7 rue de Fribourg ⓣ 022 901 13 13 Ⓦ www.charlys.com 🕐 09.00–24.00 Mon–Sat, 13.00–23.00 Sun Ⓝ Tram: 13, 15 to Cornavin

Cyber-Café 3000 This cheery café has a reliable Internet connection, plus printers and scanners. ⓐ 2 rue Henri-Christine ⓣ 022 320 74 55 Ⓦ www.cybercafe3000.ch 🕐 11.00–24.00 Mon–Fri, 14.00–24.00 Sat & Sun Ⓝ Tram: 13 to Pont-d'Arve

Las Vegas Mont-Blanc Cyberland Conveniently located near the main station. ⓐ 26 rue du Mont-Blanc ⓣ 022 738 57 44 Ⓝ Tram: 13, 15 to Cornavin

TELEPHONING SWITZERLAND
Dial 00 41 for Switzerland, then 22 for Geneva followed by the seven-digit number.

TELEPHONING ABROAD
To call out of Switzerland, simply dial 00 followed by the country code and the local number.

Directory Enquiries ⓣ 1811
International Operator ⓣ 1141

Laundrenet Doubling as a laundrette, this place offers a high-speed Internet connection, scanner and colour printing. ⓐ 83 rue de la Servette ⓣ 022 734 83 83 ⓦ www.laundrenet.com ⓛ 12.00–22.00 Mon & Wed, 09.00–22.00 Tues & Thur, 09.00–21.00 Fri & Sat, 12.00–20.00 Sun ⓝ Bus: 9 to Poterie

Phones
Geneva's modern public telephone boxes are simple to use and rates reasonable. Only some phones accept coins, so you'll probably need to buy a prepaid phonecard or use your credit card. Many of the phone booths in Geneva allow you to send SMS messages and emails also.

Post
You can purchase stamps in post offices and some newsagents. The main post office in the city centre is on rue du Mont-Blanc. ⓦ www.swisspost.ch

ELECTRICITY
Switzerland's electricity system is very reliable. It is 220 volts, 50 hertz (round, three-pin plugs). Adaptors and transformers are available for visitors.

TRAVELLERS WITH DISABILITIES
Geneva caters to travellers with special needs. Most of the city's key attractions are accessible for visitors with disabilities, including MAMCO, the Palace of Nations and the International Red Cross Museum; many offer concessions (*tarif réduit*) or free entry. If notified in advance, Swiss Federal Railways (SBB) can

assist wheelchair users and passengers with reduced mobility.
☎ 0800 007 102
Australia & New Zealand Accessibility ⓦ www.accessibility.net.au;
Disabled Persons Assembly ☎ 04 801 9100 ⓦ www.dpa.org.nz
Switzerland Mobility International Switzerland (MIS)
ⓐ Amthausquai, Olten ☎ 062 212 67 40 ⓦ www.mis-ch.ch
UK & Ireland British Council of Disabled People (BCDP)
☎ 01332 295551 ⓦ www.bcodp.org.uk
USA & Canada Society for Accessible Travel & Hospitality (SATH)
ⓐ 347 Fifth Avenue, New York ☎ 212 447 7284 ⓦ www.sath.org;
Access-Able ⓦ www.access-able.com

TOURIST INFORMATION
Geneva Tourism ⓐ 18 rue du Mont-Blanc ☎ 022 909 70 00
ⓦ www.geneve-tourisme.ch ⓛ 10.00–18.00 Mon, 09.00–18.00
Tues–Sat, 10.00–16.00 Sun
Lausanne Tourism ⓐ 9 place de la Gare ☎ 021 613 73 73
ⓦ www.lausanne-tourisme.ch ⓛ 09.00–19.00; also at Ouchy
ⓐ Place de la Navigation ⓛ 09.00–19.00 daily (Apr–Sept);
09.00–18.00 daily (Oct–Mar)
Annecy Tourist Office ⓐ 1 rue Jean-Jaurès ☎ 04 50 45 00 33
ⓦ www.lac-annecy.com ⓛ 09.00–12.00, 13.45–18.00 Mon–Sat
Carouge Tourist Information ⓦ www.carouge.ch

Emergencies

EMERGENCY NUMBERS

The following are national free emergency numbers:

Police ☎ 117
Fire ☎ 118
Ambulance ☎ 144
Emergency ☎ 112
Breakdown ☎ 140
On-call doctors ☎ 022 748 49 50

When you dial the Europe-wide emergency number ☎ 112, ask for the service you require and give details of where you are, what the emergency is and the number of the phone you are using. The operator will connect you to the service you need.

MEDICAL SERVICES

It is strongly recommended to have a valid health insurance policy before travelling to Switzerland. EU citizens are entitled to free or reduced-cost emergency healthcare with a European Health Insurance Card (EHIC). For details on late-opening pharmacies, visit ⓦ www.pharmacies-geneve.ch for a list of 24-hour pharmacies.

The centrally located **Geneva University Hospital** (HUG, ⓐ 24 rue Micheli-du-Crest ☎ 022 372 33 11 ⓦ www.hug-ge.ch) provides emergency treatment.

POLICE

Open 24 hours a day, seven days a week, the police station at Gare de Cornavin can be reached by calling ☎ 022 388 61 00

EMERGENCY PHRASES

Help!	**Fire!**	**Stop!**
Au secours!	Au feu!	Stop!
Ossercoor!	*Oh fur!*	*Stop!*

Call an ambulance/a doctor/the police/the fire service!
Appelez une ambulance/un médecin/la police/les pompiers!
*Ahperleh ewn ahngbewlahngss/uhn medesang/lah poleess/
leh pompeeyeh!*

EMBASSIES & CONSULATES

Australia @ 2 chemin des Fins, Geneva ☎ 022 799 91 00
🌐 www.australia.ch 🕐 09.00–17.00 Mon–Fri
Canada @ 88 Kirchenfeldstrasse, Bern ☎ 031 357 32 00
🌐 www.bern.gc.ca 🕐 08.00–12.00, 13.00–17.00 Mon–Thur,
08.00–13.30 Fri
Ireland @ 68 Kirchenfeldstrasse, Bern ☎ 031 352 14 42
🌐 www.embassyofireland.ch 🕐 09.00–17.00 Mon–Fri
South Africa @ 29 Alpenstrasse, Bern ☎ 031 350 13 13
🌐 www.southafrica.ch 🕐 08.00–12.30, 13.30–17.15 Mon–Thur,
08.00–12.00, 13.00–14.00 Fri
UK @ 50 Thunstrasse, Bern ☎ 031 359 77 00 🌐 www.british
embassy.ch 🕐 08.30–12.30, 13.30–17.00 Mon–Fri
USA @ 19 Sulgeneckstrasse, Bern ☎ 031 357 70 11 🌐 http://bern.
usembassy.gov 🕐 09.00–12.00, 13.30–17.30 Mon–Fri

ACKNOWLEDGEMENTS

Thomas Cook Publishing wishes to thank the photographers, picture libraries and other organisations, to whom the copyright belongs, for the photographs in this book:

Andy Christiani, pages 5, 15, 16, 32, 40–41, 63, 75, 78–9, 92 & 103; Paul Downey, page 23; Dreamstime (Lffile, page 5); Teresa Fisher, pages 9, 21, 43 & 47; istockphoto (Stevegeer, page 26; repistu, page 101; naumoid, page 119); Manotel, page 37; Tom Taylor, page 127; World Pictures/Photoshot, pages 115 & 116; Jonathan Smith, all others.

Project editor: Jennifer Jahn
Copy editor: Monica Guy
Layout: Donna Pedley
Proofreaders: Karolin Thomas & Jan McCann

Send your thoughts to
books@thomascook.com

- **Found a great bar, club, shop or must-see sight that we don't feature?**

- **Like to tip us off about any information that needs a little updating?**

- **Want to tell us what you love about this handy little guidebook and more importantly how we can make it even handier?**

Then here's your chance to tell all! Send us ideas, discoveries and recommendations today and then look out for your valuable input in the next edition of this title.

Email the above address (stating the title) or write to:
pocket guides Series Editor, Thomas Cook Publishing, PO Box 227, Coningsby Road, Peterborough PE3 8SB, UK.